WORLD CUP

1930 – 2010

-AczeL-

SPORTS
BOOKS

1930 URUGUAY

URUGUAY (LEFT) AND ARGENTINA ARE LED OUT BY THEIR CAPTAINS, JOSE NASAZZI AND MANUEL FERREIRA

1930 URUGUAY

THE FIRST WORLD CUP had been a long time coming. FIFA had been discussing having an international tournament since 1905 but until 1930 the Olympics had always provided the 'world championship'. The new competition was the brainchild of two Frenchmen: Jules Rimet, after whom the trophy was later named, and Henri Delaunay.

And it was fitting that the small South American country, whose later team manager Ondino Viera memorably said that 'other countries have their history; Uruguay has its football', should stage the first World Cup.

They were awarded it after Italy, Holland, Spain and Sweden had dropped out of the race, but having won the Olympic gold medal in 1924 and retained it in 1928, they were worthy hosts. They promised to pay all expenses and build a new stadium.

The tournament got off to a shaky start. The four UK teams were invited but, having fallen out with FIFA over broken-time payments for amateurs at the Olympics, they decided not to go, as did four other top European nations. Indeed, none of the countries who had put in a bid for the tournament decided it was worth their while travelling.

There were 13 teams in all, and this was the only World Cup where qualification was not necessary.

THE SS CONTE VERDE WHICH TRANSPORTED JULES RIMET, HIS TROPHY, THREE REFEREES AND THREE EUROPEAN TEAMS, PICKING UP THE BRAZILIANS IN RIO EN ROUTE

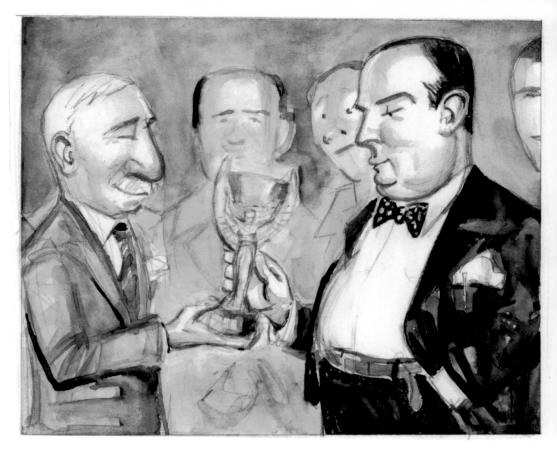

JULES RIMET (LEFT) AND
URUGUAYAN PRESIDENT
DR RAUL JUANDE
EXAMINE THE TROPHY

As well as the host nation and the four European teams who did travel – Belgium, France, Romania and Yugoslavia – there was the USA, Brazil, Argentina, Mexico, Chile, Bolivia, Paraguay and Peru. These were split into four groups with the seeds being Uruguay, Brazil, Argentina and the USA. In those days the USA were much stronger internationally than they are today.

Of course this was a World Cup of firsts, how could it not be? And in Group 3 came the first sending off, Plácido Galindo of Peru being dismissed against Romania.

The Uruguayans were desperate to do well and they dropped goalkeeper Andrés Mazali before the first game because he broke the curfew to visit his wife! Their first game was a nervous 1-0 victory against Peru, the second a 4-0 thrashing of Romania.

The USA's match with Paraguay saw the World Cup's first hat-trick – although Bert Patenaude of the United States had been dead for more than 30 years when it was finally acknowledged by FIFA.

THE SOLID GOLD CUP WHICH
LATER BECAME KNOWN AS
THE JULES RIMET TROPHY
AND WAS GIVEN TO BRAZIL
AFTER THEIR THIRD
VICTORY IN 1970

THE ESTADIO CENTENARIO WAS NOT FINISHED IN TIME FOR THE OPENING OF THE WORLD CUP

ANDRADE, URUGUAY'S BEST PLAYER.

An effort by Stábile two days later was originally recognised but Tom Florie's goal in the US match against Paraguay was reattributed to Patenaude in 2006.

Both Uruguay and Argentina won their semi-finals 6-1 which meant huge local interest in the final. Around 15,000 Argentinians set off but many were still at sea when the game kicked off.

Uruguay were not the force they had been at the previous two Olympics. Their team was ageing but it was still powerful with the influential right-half José Andrade, international football's first black player, its linchpin.

Monti, by now infamous, was picked by Argentina despite receiving death threats on the eve of the match. Not surprising then that referee, Belgian Jean Langenus, agreed to officiate only a few hours before the game and insisted there would be a boat waiting an hour after the game, just in case.

LEADING SCORER
GUILLERMO STABILE (ARGENTINA)
8 goals

LUCIEN LAURENT, OF FRANCE, ETCHED IN HISTORY AS THE SCORER OF THE FIRST GOAL AT A WORLD CUP FINALS...

1st WORLD CUP GOAL

... AND THIS WAS HOW IT HAPPENED

13 JULY, 1930   ESTADIO POCITOS   19TH MINUTE

URUGUAY WORLD CUP WINNERS 1930. (BACK ROW, LEFT TO RIGHT); FIGOLI (TRAINER),
ALVARO GESTIDO, JOSE NASAZZI, ENRIQUE BALLESTEROS, ERNESTO MASCHERONI, JOSE ANDRADE,
LORENZO FERNANDEZ

GO OUT AND ENJOY YOURSELVES...

URUGUAYAN COACH ALBERTO SUPPICI BELIEVED HIS PLAYERS SHOULD PLAY WITH FREEDOM AND SELF-EXPRESSION

THE FINAL 30 July 1930

URUGUAY 4 - 2 ARGENTINA

Estadio Centenario, Montevideo
Uruguay Attendance: 80,000
Referee: John Langenus (Belgium)

BECAUSE THERE WAS NOTHING IN THE RULES TO STIPULATE WHICH BALL WAS USED IN THE FINAL, TWO BALLS WERE USED AFTER ARGENTINA PROTESTED. THE ARGENTINIAN BALL WAS USED IN THE FIRST HALF AND THE URUGUAYAN IN THE SECOND

1-0 DORADO SHOOTS THROUGH BOTASSO'S LEGS

12th minute

1-1 PEUCELLE EQUALISES

20th minute

1-2 STABILE CELEBRATES

37th minute

2-2 CEA SCORES WITH A LOW SHOT

57th minute

3-2

SANTOS IRIARTE FROM 30 YARDS

68th minute

4-2 CASTRO HEADS HOME

89th minute

URUGUAY CHAMPIONS

ACZEL

1934 ITALY

ITALY NEEDED EXTRA TIME BEFORE
THEY BEAT CZECHOSLOVAKIA

1934 ITALY

A TOE HAVING BEEN DIPPED INTO THE WATER, the world wanted to rush in four years later. Italy were hosts and their Fascist government under Benito Mussolini did everything possible to guarantee a home victory. Italy succeeded.

England, Scotland, Wales and Northern Ireland still had issues with FIFA, with the English being convinced that all they had to do to win was to turn up. This patronising attitude was not to be tested until 1950 and then it was found to be foolish.

But 32 countries did enter – with one notable absentee. Uruguay, upset that the more powerful nations had not come to their party, decided not to enter.

This time there were qualifying groups, although there still had to be a play-off in Naples between Mexico and the USA to determine the last place.

Only European teams reached the last eight. Italy faced Spain with the result a rough 1-1 draw. For the replay Italy made four changes, one forced because Pizziolo had broken his leg to be replaced by Ferrari. In contrast Spain were able to pick only four players from the first match. A headed goal from Giuseppe Meazza was enough to put Italy through as the refereeing of Switzerland's Rene Mercet was inadequate. His display, in which he ruled out two Spanish goals for offside, led to his suspension by his own refereeing association.

Austria overcame neighbours Hungary in a brutal game in Bologna. Austrian manager Hugo Meisl called it 'a brawl'. One Hungarian was sent off while Austria's Johann Horvath was injured and missed the semi-final.

Italy's determination to succeed meant they were loaded with players from the first tournament, even though the Azzurri had not been there. Lining up at centre half was Monti, just as fierce in the tackle four years later, while on the left wing was Raimundo Orsi, who scored twice against the USA. Atilio Demaria and Enrico Guaita made up the quartet. They were the oriundi, players of Italian descent now returned from South America.

The final was a contrast of styles; power and stamina were with Italy but the Czechs favoured the 'Danubian' style of football, quick inter-passing. Italy won through though and the next finals would be in France. Would it be three home victories in a row?

ITALIAN INSIDE FORWARD
AND LEGEND GIUSEPPE
MEAZZA WAS SO GOOD
THEY NAMED AC MILAN'S
STADIUM AFTER HIM

ITALY WORLD CUP WINNERS 1934. (BACK ROW, LEFT TO RIGHT) GIAMPIERO COMBI, LUISITO MONTI, ATTILIO FERRARIS IV, LUIGI ALLEMANDI, ENRICO GUAITA, GIOVANNI FERRARI

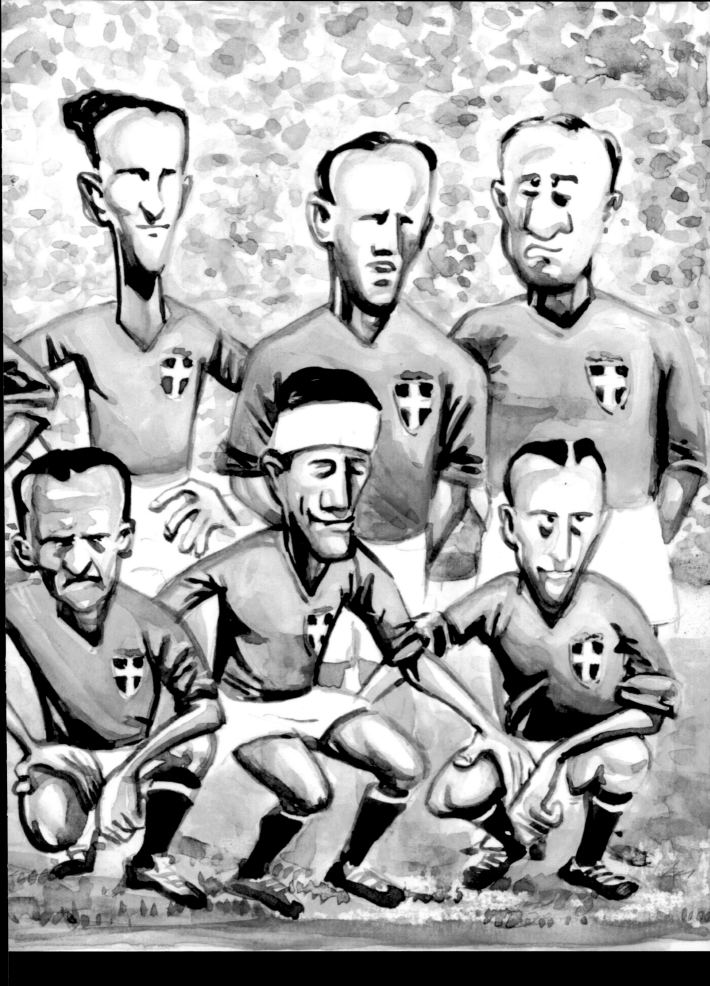

(FRONT) ANGELO SCHIAVIO, GIUSEPPE MEAZZA, ERALDO MONZEGLIO, LUIGI BERTOLINI, RAIMONDO ORSI

SEVERAL MATCHES WERE PLAYED BEFORE VERY SMALL CROWDS

MEAZZA SCORES ITALY'S VITAL GOAL IN THEIR
QUARTER-FINAL REPLAY WITH SPAIN

GOLDEN SHOE WINNER OLDRICH NEJEDLY OF
CZECHOSLOVAKIA WITH FIVE GOALS

THIS WAS THE GOALKEEPER'S WORLD CUP. THE BEST KNOWN WAS RICARDO ZAMORA OF SPAIN, ONE OF FOOTBALL'S MOST COLOURFUL CHARACTERS

ITALIAN COACH VITTORIO POZZO WAS FAMOUS FOR HIS METICULOUS PREPARATION

THE FINAL 10 June 1934

CZECHOSLOVAKIA 1 - 2 (a.e.t) ITALY

Stadio Nazionale PNF, Rome
Attendance: 55,000
Referee: Ivan Eklind (Sweden)

COMBI

MONZEGLIO   ALLEMANDI

FERRARIS   MONTI   BERTOLINI
        MEAZA   FERRARI

GUAITA   SCHIAVO   ORSI

PUC   SOBOTKA   JUNEK
    NEJEDLY   SVOBODA

KRCIL   CAMBAL   KOSTÁLEK

CTYROKY   ZENISEK

PLÁNICKA

THIS WAS THE ONLY TIME TWO GOAL-KEEPERS HAVE CAPTAINED THEIR COUNTRIES IN A WORLD CUP FINAL

55th minute

PUC FAILS TO WIN A PENALTY...

AND THEN HE IS CARRIED OFF INJURED

0-1 PUC COMES BACK TO SCORE!

76th minute

1-1 ORSI EQUALISES

81st minute

EXTRA-TIME

SCHIAVIO SCORES THE WINNER FROM FOUR YARDS

95th minute

2 - 1 ITALY ARE CHAMPIONS

1938 FRANCE

1938 FRANCE

**SURELY EVERYONE WOULD AGREE that the third World Cup deserved to be held in France – the
country of Jules Rimet and Henri Delaunay, the men whose brainchild the competition was?**

Everyone except South America, it seems. Brazil were the only team from the continent to travel to France
although Cuba, in the tournament because Mexico had pulled out, and Dutch East Indies were included in
the first round. But Uruguay and Argentina were not the only high-profile absentees. Europe was on the edge
of an abyss; the Second World War was brewing. Spain were missing because the country was enveloped in
a civil war; Austria, although qualified, were missing because the country had been annexed by
Germany.

And none of the four United Kingdom nations were there; they were still sniffily
out of sorts with FIFA.

The Brazilians gave a glimpse of the riches to come in future tournaments and
their star Leonidas struck a hat-trick as the South Americans triumphed 6-5 over
Poland after extra time. But he was outdone by Ernest Wilimowski, who became
the first man to net four goals in a World Cup match and still finished on the
losing side.

After a slow start, Italy went from strength to strength. They put out France
in the quarter-finals played before 59,000 spectators at an enlarged Stade
Colombes.

This was the roughest World Cup so far and the quarter-final between Brazil and
Czechoslovakia produced mayhem with three sendings off – Zezé Procópio and Machado
of Brazil and Jan Riha of Czechoslovakia – and two fractured limbs in their 1-1 draw. Goalkeeper
František Plánicka suffered a broken arm and forward Oldrich Nejedlý a broken leg, in his case after equalising
Leonidas's opening goal. The Czechs finished with nine players, Brazil with eight.

Leonidas was one of only two Brazilians retained for the replay and he scored the equaliser in a 2-1 win
that took the South Americans to their first semi-final.

Leonidas was missing from the semi-final with Italy, who won 2-1 in a disappointing game.

The 4-2 scoreline to Italy in the final suggests almost a mismatch but this would do the Hungarians an
injustice although the Azzurri, wearing their usual blue shirts for the final, retained their title.

YVES, THE GRANDSON OF JULES RIMET, MAKES THE DRAW FOR THE TOURNAMENT AS HIS
PROUD GRANDFATHER STEADIES THE JAR

SIM

BRASIL

BRAZIL WAS THE ONLY SOUTH
AMERICAN COUNTRY TO AGREE
TO PLAY IN 1938

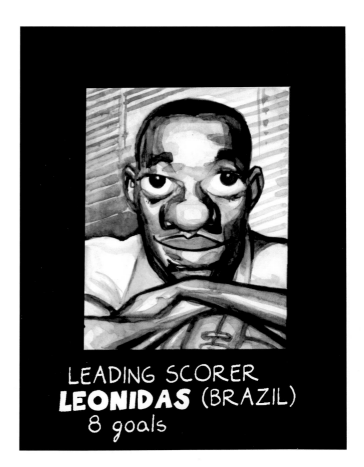

LEADING SCORER
LEONIDAS (BRAZIL)
8 goals

THE GREAT CZECH GOALKEEPER
FRANTISEK PLANICKA PLAYED ON
WITH A BROKEN ARM

COLAUSSI'S CLASSIC QUARTER-FINAL GOAL FOR ITALY AGAINST FRANCE. NOTE THAT THE ITALIANS ARE WEARING BLACK SHIRTS

THE GERMAN TEAM'S NAZI SALUTE WAS GREETED WITH JEERS IN FRANCE

ITALY WORLD CUP WINNERS 1938. (BACK ROW, LEFT TO RIGHT) BURLANDO (CO-TRAINER),
AMEDEO BIAVATI, VACCARO (FIGC PRESIDENT), VITTORIO POZZO (COACH),
ANGELI (MASSEUR, HALF HIDDEN) SILVIO PIOLA, GIOVANNI FERRARI, GINO COLAUSSI

(FRONT) UGO LOCATELLI, GUISEPPE MEAZZA, ALFREDO FONI, PIETRO SERANTONI (LYING)
ALDO OLIVIERI, PIETRO RAVA, MICHELE ANDREOLO (MASSEUR)

GIUSEPPE MEAZZA WON HIS SECOND
WORLD CUP IN 1938...

THE FINAL 19 June 1938

ITALY 4-2 HUNGARY

Stade Olympique de Colombes, Paris
Attendance: 60,000
Referee: Georges Capdeville (France)

...AS DID VITTORIO POZZO,
THE GREAT ITALIAN COACH

OLIVIERI
FONI   RAVA
SERANTONI   ANDREOLO   LOCATELLI
        MEAZA   FERRARI
BIAVATI   PIOLA   COLAUSSI

TITKOS   SÁROSI   SAS
    ZSENGELLÉR   VINCZE
LÁZÁR   SZÚCS   SZALAY
    BIRÓ   POLGAR
            SZABÓ

1-0 PIOLA PASS, COLAUSSI SCORES

1-1 TITKOS EQUALISES

2-1 PIOLA SCORES

3-1 COLAUSSI SCORES A BRILLIANT SECOND

3-2 SAROSI FOR HUNGARY

4-2 PIOLA MAKES THE GAME SAFE

The Italians are World Champions

1950 BRAZIL

THE MIGHTY MARACANA, THE WORLD'S BIGGEST STADIUM. NOT QUITE FINISHED IN TIME FOR THE 1950 WORLD CUP BUT VERY IMPRESSIVE ALL THE SAME

1950 BRAZIL

THE WORLD CUP TOOK FIVE YEARS TO RETURN after the carnage of the Second World War and it was back to South America and Brazil. This time England competed. The Home Nations had returned to FIFA in 1946 but there were still high-profile withdrawals. Scotland refused to go in a fit of pique because they had finished second in the Home Nations tournament. And there was no Argentina, no Czechoslovakia, no France.

Controversially it was decided to play the competition in pools – Henri Delaunay resigned from the World Cup Committee in protest – and it was luck not judgement that declared that the final game in the tournament would decide the winners.

Brazil also upset the other teams by playing all but one of their six games in Rio while the others trooped around the huge country. Portugal refused to take Scotland's place so there were only 13 teams involved when the finals began. It meant that in one pool there was only Uruguay and Bolivia. Amazingly, the powers that be did not re-organise the groups.

Italy's dominance was destroyed by the Superga air disaster in 1949 when the entire Torino team was killed when their plane, returning from a friendly in Lisbon, crashed into the wall of a monastery. They included eight of the Azzurri.

After an undistinguished 2-0 win over Chile England suffered one of the biggest shocks In World Cup history. Their team of full-time professionals was beaten 1-0 by the part-timers from the USA.

The final pool contained Brazil, Sweden, Spain and Uruguay and by happy accident it came down to the final game – Brazil v Uruguay. The venue was the mighty Maracanã, a brute of a stadium designed to hold 200,000.

Every Brazilian was sure that there was no way they could lose. Uruguay would be torn to shreds by the inside forward trio of Zizinho, Ademir and Jair. Behind them was the powerful Bauer.

Uruguay, though, had the massive Valera in defence and he was helped by a man with a famous name, Andrade, the nephew of one of the stalwarts of the team which won the competition in 1930. Then there was Maspoli, an acrobatic and resilient goalkeeper, who kept a rampant Brazil at bay until just after half-time. But Uruguay did not crumble and replied with two second half-goals.

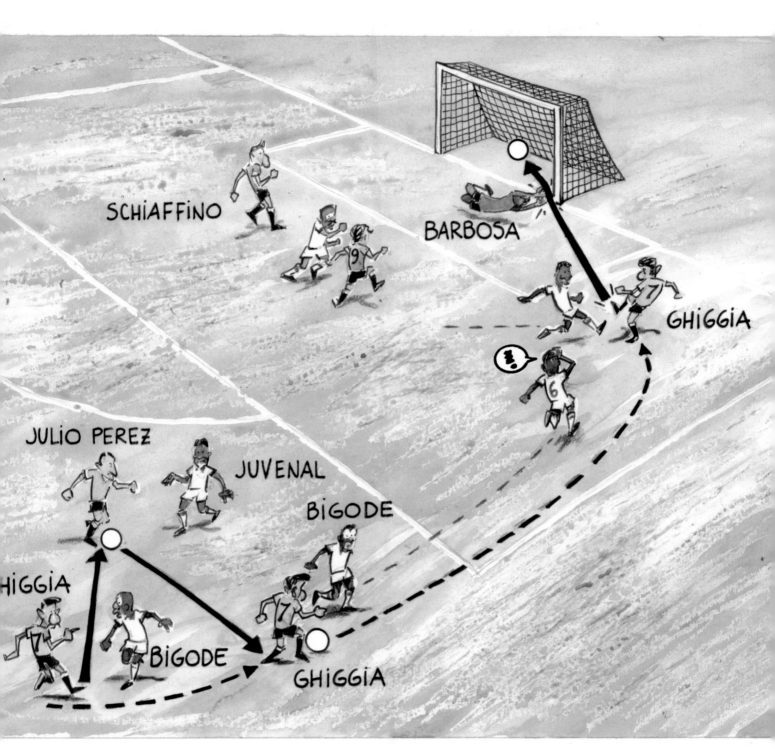

URUGUAY'S WINNING GOAL SCORED BY ALCIDES GHIGGIA IN THE 'FINAL' THAT WASN'T

-ACZEL

THE ENGLISH PLAYERS
WATCHING BEACH
FOOTBALL AT
COPACABANA...

...WHILE ALF RAMSEY CAN
ONLY WATCH AS JOE
GAETJENS SCORES THE
ONLY GOAL OF THE GAME
IN ENGLAND'S HUMILIATION
BY THE USA

ADEMIR WAS THE GOLDEN SHOE
WINNER WITH EIGHT GOALS BUT
FINISHED ON THE LOSING SIDE

ALTHOUGH 174,000 FANS PAID TO GET INTO
THE FINAL MATCH BETWEEN BRAZIL AND
URUGUAY IT WAS ESTIMATED ANOTHER
30,000 GOT IN WITHOUT TICKETS. IT WAS
A MIRACLE NO ONE WAS HURT

URUGUAY WORLD CUP WINNERS 1950. (BACK ROW, LEFT TO RIGHT) OBDULIO VARELA, JUAN LOPEZ (COACH), EUSEBIO TEJERA, VASQUEZ (ASSISTANT COACH), ABATE (ASSISTANT COACH), SCHUBERT GAMBETTA, MATIAS GONZALES, GASTON MASPOLI, VICTOR ANDRADE

(FRONT) KIRCHBERG (MASSEUR), ALCIDES GHIGGIA, JULIO PEREZ, OSCAR MIGUEZ, JUAN SCHIAFFINO, RUBEN MORAN, FIGOLI (ASSISTANT COACH)

OBDULIO VARELA, URUGUAY'S
CAPTAIN IN BULLISH MOOD
AFTER THE FINAL GAME WITH
BRAZIL THAT GAVE HIS TEAM
THE TROPHY

JUAN LOPEZ, THE URUGUAYAN COACH, GAVE
HIS TEAM PRECISE INSTRUCTIONS ON HOW TO
BEAT BRAZIL

FINAL MATCH 16 JULY 1950

URUGUAY 2-1 BRAZIL

Estdio do Maracan, Rio de Janeiro
Attendance: 174,000
Referee: George Reader (England)

0 - 1 FRIACA (RIGHT) SCORES 47TH MINUTE

1 - 1 SCHIAFFINO VOLLEY

66TH MINUTE

2 - 1 GHIGGIA DRIBBLES THROUGH AND SHOOTS... 79TH MINUTE

①

...INTO THE BOTTOM CORNER

②

GOOAAL! AND AN ABSOLUTE TRAGEDY FOR BRAZIL

③

THERE WAS NO OFFICIAL CEREMONY PLANNED TO HAND OVER
THE CUP TO URUGUAY... BUT THEY WEREN'T WORRIED.
ALL THAT MATTERED WAS THAT THEY'D WON.

1954 SWITZERLAND

THE 1954 WORLD CUP WILL BE
REMEMBERED FOR THE RAIN AND
FOR THE BRUTALITY OF SOME
OF ITS MATCHES

1954 SWITZERLAND

THE ORGANISERS HAD ANOTHER SYSTEM for the 1954 tournament held in Switzerland. It was not as daft as that used four years before but it was odd nevertheless. Two teams in each of the four groups were seeded and they did not have to play each other. They played only the unseeded teams.

The holders Brazil were in Group 1 but the overwhelming favourites were in Group 2. Hungary had won the 1952 Helsinki Olympics and they had just beaten England 6-3 at Wembley and 7-1 in the Nep Stadium. And with Ferenc Puskás, Sándor Kocsis and Nándor Hidegkuti revolutionising the game, they beat Korea 9-0 and West Germany 8-3 in their opening group.

But the game with Germany had a hugely significant effect on the rest of the competition. Liebrich fouled Puskás with half an hour left and the Hungarian talisman was never properly fit after that.

Hungary and Brazil were involved in one of the most brutal matches ever seen in the World Cup. It is still remembered as 'the Battle of Berne'. Three players were sent off. József Bozsik, a deputy in the Hungarian parliament, and Nilton Santos swapped punches while Humberto Tozzi kicked Gyula Lóránt. But it was the mayhem after Hungary won 4-2 that gave the match its notoriety. Some say Puskás, who was not playing, started it by hitting Pinheiro with a bottle, but certainly the Brazilians invaded the Hungarian dressing room and the Hungarian coach Gusztáv Sebes suffered a wound to his cheek.

Hungary's semi-final with Uruguay was one of the all-time great World Cup matches. It was 2-2 after 90 minutes and Hungary, again without Puskás, prevailed 4-2. The second semi pitted West Germany against an Austrian side who fell apart to lose 6-1, five of the winning team's goals coming in the second half.

So West Germany faced Hungary. Having lost so heavily in the opening group stages Germany surely had no hope. But Hungary made the mistake of playing Puskás, despite his injury, and although the 'galloping major' put his team ahead after six minutes he was generally ineffective. The Germans kept their heads as the rain lashed down and although Puskás had a goal disallowed Germany prevailed.

HUNGARY'S FERENC PUSKAS WAS EXPECTED
TO BE THE STAR OF THE TOURNAMENT
BUT INJURY STOPPED HIM FROM BEING AS
EFFECTIVE AS USUAL

CAPTAIN FRITZ WALTER (LEFT), HORST ECKEL AND COACH SEPP HERBERGER ARE CARRIED
ON THE SHOULDERS OF GERMANY'S TRIUMPHANT FANS

HELMUT RAHN

SCORED TWICE IN THE FINAL...

...INCLUDING HIS BRILLIANT WINNER

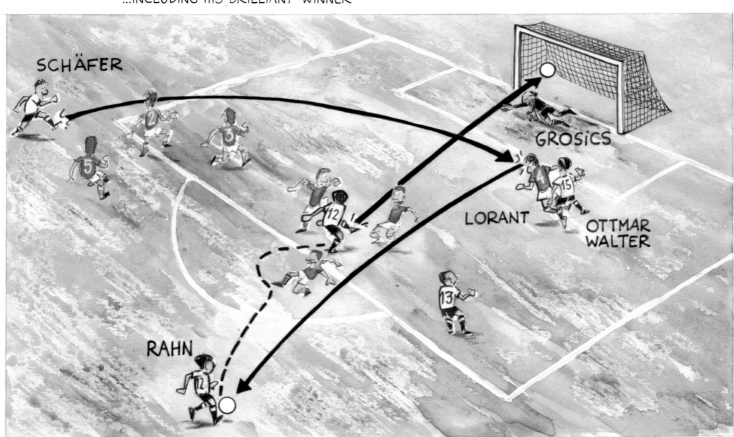

FRITZ WALTER,
THE GERMAN CAPTAIN

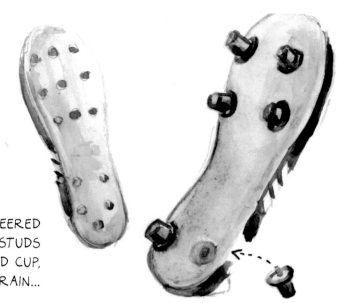

THE GERMANS PIONEERED
SCREW-IN STUDS
AT THE WORLD CUP,
HOPING FOR RAIN...

...AND THEIR PRAYERS WERE ANSWERED IN THE FINAL!

SANDOR KOCSIS
OF HUNGARY WON
THE GOLDEN SHOE
WITH 11 GOALS

1954

WEST GERMANY WORLD CUP WINNERS 1954. (BACK ROW, LEFT TO RIGHT) SEPP HERBERGER (COACH), FRITZ WALTER, HELMUT RAHN, JUPP POSIPAL, HORST ECKEL, WERNER LIEBRICH, OTTMAR WALTER

(FRONT) KARL MAI, TONI TUREK, WERNER KOHLMEYER

GERMAN RADIO COMMENTATOR HERBERT ZIMMERMANN
MADE HIMSELF A HOUSEHOLD NAME
WITH HIS COMMENTARY ON THE
FINAL. BUT THE TOURNAMENT
WAS THE FIRST TO BE TELEVISED
AND THAT WOULD BECOME THE DOMINANT MEDIUM

THE FINAL 4 JULY 1954

W GERMANY 3 - 2 HUNGARY

Wankdorf Stadium, Berne
Attendance: 64,000
Referee: William Ling (England)

0-1 PUSKAS SCORES - POWERFUL AND ELEGANT

0-2 CZIBOR TAKES ADVANTAGE OF TUREK AND KOHLMEYER'S MISUNDERSTANDING

1-2 MORLOCK TOE POKES THE BALL INTO THE NET AFTER A CROSS FROM RAHN

2-2 RAHN SCORES AFTER A CORNER FROM FRITZ WALTER

HELMUT RAHN GRABS HIS SECOND AND GERMANY'S WINNER IN THE 84TH MINUTE

3-2

1958 SWEDEN

AT 17 PELE BECAME A WORLD STAR IN SWEDEN AS BRAZIL WON THE WORLD CUP FOR THE FIRST TIME

1958 SWEDEN

SO FAR NO TEAM HAD WON THE WORLD CUP OUTSIDE THEIR OWN CONTINENT: that was to change in Sweden when Brazil at last realised their huge potential and introduced to the world a teenager who was to become the greatest player ever seen – Edson Arantes do Nascimento, thankfully known as Pelé.

The tournament, the first to be shown widely on television, featured all four of the Home Nations. They'd all qualified, for the first and only time, but England were suffering from the massive handicap of losing players like captain Roger Byrne, the colossus Duncan Edwards and centre forward Tommy Taylor, who had been killed in the Munich air crash in February 1958.

It was Wales and Northern Ireland, the two smallest countries in the tournament, who were the best of the Home Nations. Wales beat Hungary, shorn of men like Puskás and Kocsis, 2-1 in a play-off to get through to the knockout stage while Northern Ireland beat Czechoslovakia in another play-off to reach the same stage. It took a deflected goal from Pelé for Brazil to put out Wales but Northern Ireland were stricken by injury and went out 4-0 to France with Fontaine getting two.

It was a pity that the free-scoring French had to face Brazil in the last four. With Fontaine being serviced by Kopa, a member of European champions Real Madrid's glittering forward line and that year's European Footballer of the Year, France outscored even Brazil with 23 goals. Their semi-final was the game of the tournament. Fontaine equalised Vavá's early opener but a second goal from Didi gave the South Americans a half-time lead. After half-time Pelé came into his own with a hat-trick and Brazil were through 5-2.

The other semi was between the hosts and the reigning champions West Germany. Erich Juskowiak became the first ever German player to be sent off in an international game, and with captain Fritz Walter suffering an injury Sweden went through 3-1.

About the only thing that spoiled Brazil's party on the day of the final was that they had to wear blue shirts to avoid a clash with Sweden. They had arrived without an alternative kit and had to buy the blue one and sew on the badges from their usual yellow shirts. They have worn blue away shirts ever since.

FRENCH STRIKER
JUSTE FONTAINE WON
THE GOLDEN SHOE
WITH 13 GOALS –
STILL A TOURNAMENT
RECORD

FONTAINE'S GOAL AGAINST BRAZIL WAS A CLASSIC BUT IT WAS IN A LOSING CAUSE

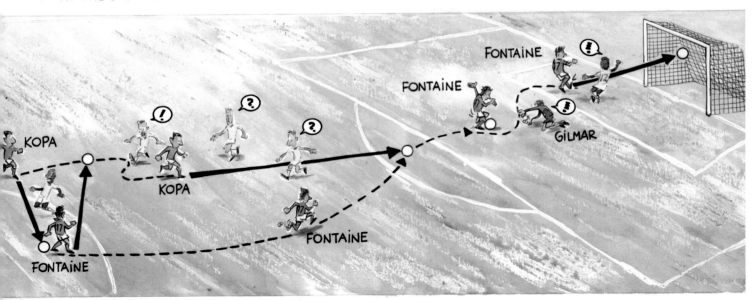

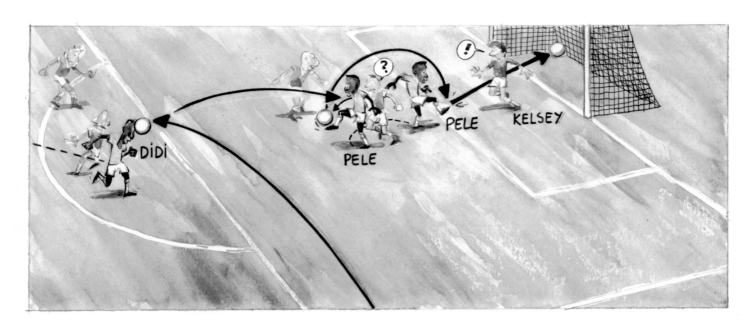

AGAINST TINY WALES BRAZIL RELIED ON ONE GOAL FROM THEIR TEENAGE STAR...

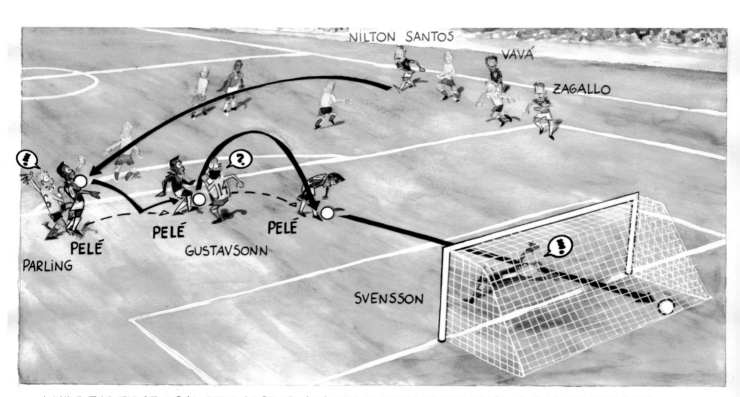

...WHILE THE FIRST GOAL PELE SCORED AGAINST SWEDEN IN THE FINAL IS ONE OF THE BEST WORLD CUP GOALS, IF NOT THE BEST

(RIGHT) EDSON ARANTES DO NASCIMENTO
OR "O REI"
OR, SIMPLY PELE

BRAZIL WORLD CUP WINNERS 1958. (BACK ROW, LEFT TO RIGHT) VICENTE FEOLA (COACH),
DJALMA SANTOS, ZITO, BELLINI, NILTON SANTOS, ORLANDO, GILMAR

(FRONT) GARRINCHA DIDI PELE VAVA ZAGALLO AMARAL (ASSISTANT COACH)

PELE WAS IN TEARS AT THE END OF THE FINAL. HE WAS TO BECOME AND REMAIN THE WORLD'S GREATEST EVER PLAYER

THE FINAL 29 June 1958

SWEDEN 2 - 5 BRAZIL

Rsunda Stadium, Solna
Attendance: 51,800
Referee: Maurice Guigue (France)

VICENTE FEOLA DREAMS UP HIS REVOLUTIONARY 4-4-2 SYSTEM

1962 CHILE

GARRINCHA BAMBOOZLES THE DEFENCE AS BRAZIL RETAIN THE WORLD CUP THEY WON IN SWEDEN FOUR YEARS EARLIER

1962 CHILE

BRAZIL DID NOT HAVE SO FAR TO TRAVEL FOUR YEARS LATER to defend their trophy – just a hop across the Andes to Chile, although they had to do it mostly without Pelé, who limped out of the second game against Czechoslovakia with an injury to his left thigh. Brazil brought in Amarildo, quickly nicknamed 'the white Pele', but the star of their overall victory was Garrincha. The 'Little Bird' – Garrincha literally means 'wren' in Portuguese – was 25 and at the height of his considerable powers.

Brazil still had nine of their 1958 team in their squad although they had a new coach Aymore Moreira, brother of Zezé, the man in charge in Switzerland in 1954.

Chile undoubtedly had some of the most picturesque stadiums in the world but no one was looking at the snow-capped Andes when the host nation met Italy in the 'the Battle of Santiago'. All over the world fans stared at their television screens in disbelief.

Italy's Giorgio Ferrini and Mario David were sent off and the atmosphere suggested that violence might break out at any time. It all began with the Chileans spitting at their opponents from the start. Then Chile's Leonel Sanchez, the son of a boxer, broke Umberto Maschio's nose with a left hook that the TV cameras caught but the linesman missed. Ferrini went for hacking down Landa and then David aimed a kick at Sanchez's head. 'The most stupid, appalling, disgusting and disgraceful exhibition of football,' said the BBC. Chile won 2-0 and referee Ken Aston of England said the game was 'uncontrollable'.

England were mugged in their quarter-final by Brazil. The English defenders couldn't catch Garrincha, who scored twice in a 3-1 win, including a headed goal when the 5ft 7ins winger outjumped the 6ft 2ins centre half Maurice Norman.

In the semi-finals Brazil defeated Chile 4-2 with Garrincha and Vavá each scoring twice although the 'Little Bird' was sent off for retaliating against Rojas and Chile's Landa was also dismissed. In the other semi, Czechoslovakia won the 'slovakia' derby against the Yugolsavs 3-1, Adolf Scherer scoring twice.

Garrincha was allowed to play in the final and Brazil retained the trophy.

THE BATTLE OF SANTIAGO

"THE BATTLE OF SANTIAGO". ALTHOUGH CHILE'S LEONEL SANCHEZ TWICE PUNCHED ITALIANS, IT WAS ITALY WHO HAD TWO MEN – GIORGIO FERRINI AND MARIO DAVID – SENT OFF. "THE MOST STUPID, APPALLING, DISGUSTING AND DISGRACEFUL EXHIBITION OF FOOTBALL," SAID THE BBC. CHILE WON 2-0 AND REFEREE KEN ASTON OF ENGLAND SAID THE GAME WAS "UNCONTROLLABLE"

PELE LIMPS OUT OF THE WORLD CUP... BUT HE WOULD BE BACK AGAIN AND AGAIN

ENGLAND GOAL POACHER JIMMY GREAVES MAY HAVE SCORED ONLY ONE GOAL BUT AT LEAST HE CAUGHT A STRAY DOG AGAINST BRAZIL. GARRINCHA THOUGHT IT WAS SO FUNNY HE TOOK THE DOG HOME AS A PET!

WITH PELE INJURED, GARRINCHA "THE LITTLE BIRD" TOOK OVER AS BRAZIL'S SHINING STAR WITH HIS AMAZING DRIBBLING SKILLS, FIERCE SHOOTING AND IN ONE CASE HE OUTJUMPED THE 6FT 2INS ENGLAND CENTRE HALF MAURICE NORMAN EVEN THOUGH HE WAS ONLY 5FT 7INS

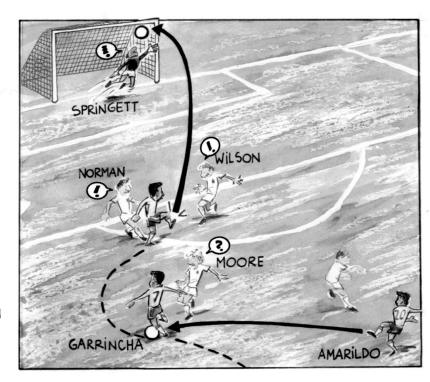

GARRINCHA'S LEFT LEG WAS 2½ INCHES SHORTER THAN HIS RIGHT

THE GARRINCHA SHOW

RAZIL WORLD CUP WINNERS 1962. (BACK ROW, LEFT TO RIGHT) AYMORE MOREIRA (TRAINER),
JALMA SANTOS, ZITO, GILMAR, ZOZIMO, NILTON SANTOS, MAURO, DR. GOSLING (TEAM DOCTOR)

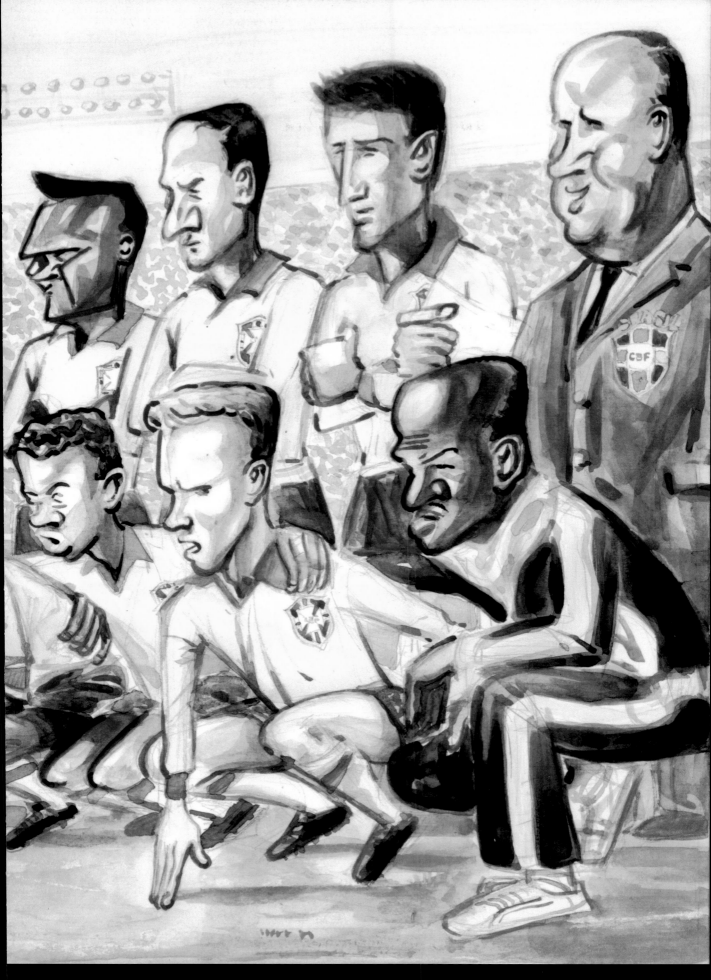

(FRONT ROW) AMERICO (MASSEUR), GARRINCHA, DIDI, VAVA, AMARILDO,
ZAGALLO, COACH

GARRINCHA AND FIVE OTHERS SHARED THE GOLDEN SHOE WITH FOUR GOALS EACH. THE OTHERS WERE (CLOCKWISE FROM BOTTOM LEFT), CHILE'S LEONEL SANCHEZ, YUGOSLAVIA'S DRAZEN JERKOVIC, THE SOVIET UNION'S VALENTIN IVANOV, HUNGARY'S FLORIAN ALBERT AND BRAZIL'S VAVA

THE FINAL 17 June 1962

BRAZIL 3 - 1 CZECHOSLOVAKIA

Estadio Nacional, Santiago
Attendance: 68,000
Referee: Nikolai Latychev (Soviet Union)

PLAYERS SHOULD ENJOY THEIR FOOTBALL

AYMORE MOREIRA, BRAZIL'S COACH, HAD A SIMPLE PHILOSOPHY ALTHOUGH HE CHANGED FROM 4-4-2 TO 4-3-3

PELE CAN ONLY WATCH THE FINAL

0-1 MASOPUST

15th minute

1-1 AMARILDO EQUALISES FOR BRAZIL FROM AN 'IMPOSSIBLE' ANGLE

17th minute

2-1 ZITO HEADS HOME AMARILDO'S CROSS

69th minute

3-1 VAVA SCORES THE THIRD AND MAKES BRAZIL WORLD CHAMPIONS

78th minute

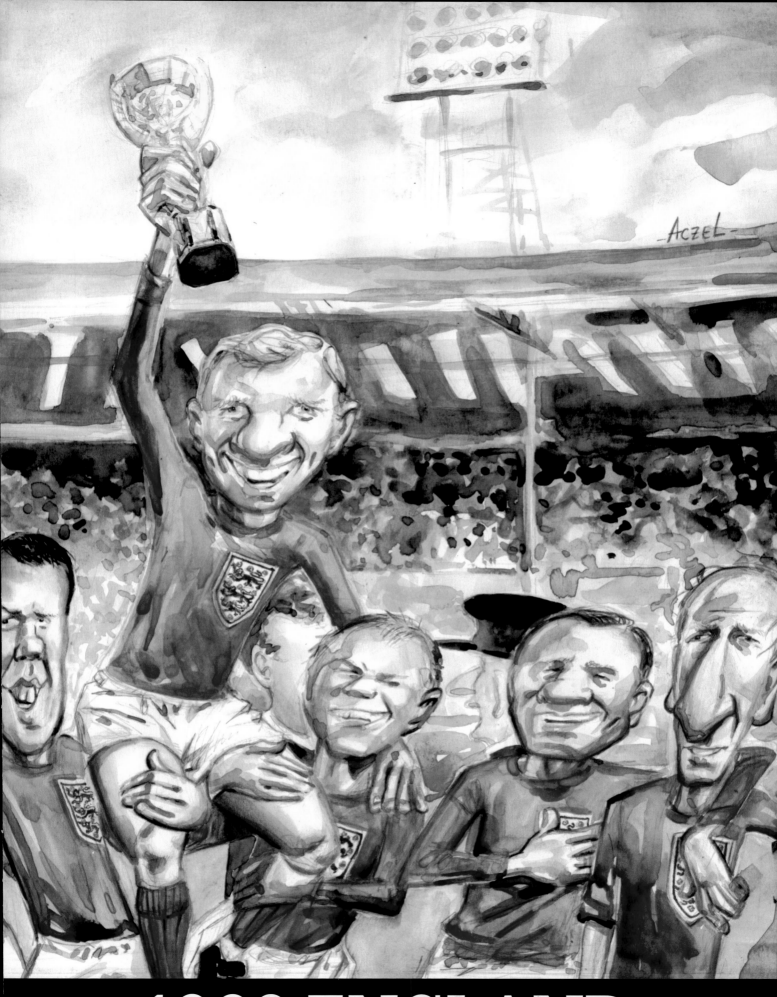

1966 ENGLAND

1966 ENGLAND

ENGLAND, THE COUNTRY THAT EXPORTED FOOTBALL to the rest of the world, got their chance to stage the World Cup only 20 years after being readmitted to FIFA.

And despite grumbles about refereeing decisions and complaints that they played all their matches at their 'home' ground of Wembley, England became the first host nation to win the tournament in 28 years.

The holders, Brazil, had Pelé again but he found he was a marked man. He was clattered by the Bulgarians and then kicked out of the competition by the Portuguese. It meant he missed the match with Hungary which was the last for Garrincha. It was the only time the 'Little Bird' finished on a losing Brazil side.

Portugal faced North Korea in the quarter-final at Goodison Park, and found themselves 3-0 down after 25 minutes. But they won 5-3 after Eusebio scored four goals to almost single-handedly drag his team to safety.

Brazil were not the only aggrieved team from South America. Argentina met England in the quarter-finals and went out 1-0 in a testy, ill-tempered match in which their captain Antonio Rattin was sent off. But he refused to leave the field, arguing furiously with German referee Rudolf Kreitlein. Neither spoke the other's language but the referee said the look on Rattin's face was enough.

The reverberations were to last for years.

West Germany won a miserable semi-final against Hungary while England faced Portugal in the other semi-final and two Bobby Charlton shots were enough for the win. Eusebio, who finished as the tournament's top scorer, scored a penalty but it was not enough.

England had to play in their red second strip against West Germany in the final and Geoff Hurst's hat-trick, the first and only one in a World Cup final, gave England the win. If his second was controversial – they are still arguing whether the ball crossed the line – the third was a classic. The unflappable Bobby Moore took the ball out of defence and spoted Hurst's run. The West Ham forward took the ball on to drive it into the roof of the net, prompting a phrase from BBC commentator Kenneth Wolstenholme which has gone into English football folklore: 'Some people are on the pitch. They think it's all over (pause as shot goes in) – it is now.'

DID THE BALL CROSS THE LINE FOR GEOFF HURST'S SECOND GOAL IN THE FINAL?
THAT'S BEEN ARGUED ABOUT FIERCELY EVER SINCE. BUT THE SOVIET LINESMAN SAID IT HAD
AND REFEREE GOTTFRIED DIENST AGREED WITH HIM

PICKLES (THE DOG NOT THE CAMERAMAN) WAS THE HERO OF THE DAY WHEN AFTER THE TROPHY
WAS STOLEN HE FOUND IT IN A GARDEN IN SOUTH-EAST LONDON

BOBBY CHARLTON SCORES AGAINST MEXICO –
ENGLAND'S FIRST GOAL OF THE COMPETITION

EUSEBIO, WITH NINE GOALS, WON THE GOLDEN SHOE.
THEY INCLUDED FOUR FOR PORTUGAL AGAINST
NORTH KOREA AT GOODISON PARK AS HE PULLED
HIS TEAM BACK FROM A 3-0 DEFICIT TO WIN 5-3

PAK DOO IK SCORES THE GOAL THAT PROVIDED ONE OF THE WORLD CUP'S BIGGEST UPSETS
AS NORTH KOREA BEAT ITALY 1-0 AND SENT THEM HOME AFTER THE GROUP STAGE

ENGLAND MANAGER ALF RAMSEY STOPS GEORGE COHEN
EXCHANGING SHIRTS AFTER THE QUARTER-FINAL WITH ARGENTINA.
RAMSEY LATER CALLED THE ARGENTINIANS "ANIMALS"

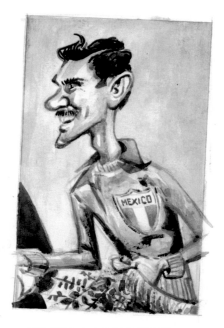

MEXICAN GOALKEEPER
ANTONIO CARBAJAL
MADE HISTORY IN 1966
WHEN PLAYING IN HIS
FIFTH WORLD CUP

PELE'S WORLD CUP WAS OVER QUICKLY AFTER BRUTAL
DISPLAYS BY BULGARIA AND PORTUGAL

BOBBY CHARLTON SCORES AGAINST
PORTUGAL IN THE SEMI-FINAL

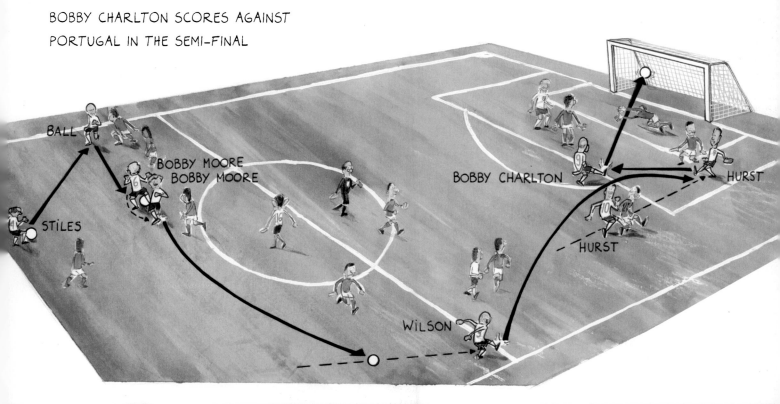

ENGLAND WORLD CUP WINNERS 1966. (BACK ROW, LEFT TO RIGHT) HAROLD SHEPHERDSON (TRAINER), NOBBY STILES, ROGER HUNT, GORDON BANKS, JACKIE CHARLTON, GEORGE COHEN, RAY WILSON, ALF RAMSEY (MANAGER).

(FRONT) MARTIN PETERS GEOFF HURST BOBBY MOORE ALAN BALL BOBBY CHARLTON

EVEN STRONG MEN WEEP. JACKIE CHARLTON SINKS TO THE TURF AFTER ENGLAND'S VICTORY

ENGLAND'S FAMOUSLY PHLEGMATIC MANAGER ALF RAMSEY SITS EMOTIONLESS ON THE ENGLAND BENCH AT THE FINAL WHISTLE AS HIS ASSISTANT HAROLD SHEPHERDSON JUMPS FOR JOY. "SIT DOWN HAROLD, YOU'RE BLOCKING MY VIEW," RAMSEY IS REPORTED TO HAVE SAID. WEST GERMAN MANAGER HELMUT SCHON (FAR LEFT) CAN'T BELIEVE HIS TEAM HAVE LOST

THE FINAL 30 July 1966

ENGLAND 4 - 2 (a.e.t) WEST GERMANY

Wembley Stadium, London
Attendance: 98,000
Referee: Gottfried Dienst (Switzerland)

ALF RAMSEY, ENGLAND MANAGER

ACZEL

1970 MEXICO

PELE IS HOISTED BY JAIRZINHO AS THEY
CELEBRATE HIS GOAL IN THE FINAL

(RIGHT) THE GREAT BRAZILIAN SWAPS
SHIRTS WITH ENGLAND CAPTAIN
BOBBY MOORE AFTER BRAZIL'S EPIC
1-0 VICTORY

1970 MEXICO

WAS THIS THE BEST WORLD CUP EVER? Won by the best team ever? Yes and yes must be the answers, although it didn't promise to be when Mexico was awarded the tournament.

'Too hot and at too high an altitude' said most countries, and it was suggested that playing the games in the middle of the day to suit European TV companies meant players would die. But the heat and height resulted in football that was more thoughtful and considered. The players couldn't make up for lack of skill with athleticism.

The result was superb attacking play, won by Brazil in the most glorious fashion imaginable. It was their third win and it meant they kept the Jules Rimet Trophy. Brazil included Pelé, who thankfully had changed his mind about never playing again in a World Cup after being kicked out of the 1966 finals. Garrincha was replaced on the right by Jairzinho a different but just as effective a winger.

England, as holders, were arguably stronger than in 1966 but manager Alf Ramsey upset local supporters which did not help and there was the problem of captain Bobby Moore having been detained in Colombia, farcically accused of stealing a bracelet. But Moore was rarely flustered as he showed in the best game of the first round, the game with Brazil. It was Gerd Müller of West Germany, scorer of successive hat-tricks against Bulgaria and Peru. who put out England in the quarter-finals. England had suffered a blow before the match when Gordon Banks suffered food poisoning and had to be replaced by Peter Bonetti. They went from 2-0 up to lose 3-2 after two mistakes by the stand-in 'keeper.

The Germans scored three times again when they met Italy in the semi-finals with Müller again scoring twice; European Footballer of the Year Gianni Rivera snatched the extra-time winner.

Italy, no mugs, faced Brazil in the final. They, too, had their stars. Burgnich and Facchetti at full-back, Boninsegna, Riva and Mazzola with Rivera on the bench.

But it was Pelé who opened the scoring with a header and despite Roberto Boninsegna's equaliser the outcome was never in doubt.

THE PERFECT TACKLE. JAIRZINHO HURTLES TOWARDS THE ENGLAND GOAL ONLY FOR BOBBY MOORE TO HALT HIM WITH A TACKLE THAT DREW GASPS FRON SPECTATORS...

...BUT THE BRAZILIAN WINGER HAD THE LAST LAUGH WHEN PELE SET HIM UP FOR THE ONLY GOAL OF THE GROUP MATCH

THE BRAZIL-ENGLAND CLASH IS ALSO REMEMBERED FOR A SAVE BY GORDON BANKS OF ENGLAND THAT IS GENERALLY RECOGNISED AS THE BEST IN WORLD CUP HISTORY. PELE'S HEADER LOOKED DESTINED FOR THE BOTTOM CORNER UNTIL, SOMEHOW, BANKS DIVED TO PALM THE BALL OVER THE BAR

WEST GERMANY'S GOAL MACHINE GERD MULLER WON THE GOLDEN SHOE WITH TEN GOALS. HERE HE STRIKES TO BEAT ENGLAND'S STAND-IN GOALKEEPER PETER BONETTI AND SEND THE REIGNING CHAMPIONS HOME AFTER THE QUARTER-FINALS

THE 1970 WORLD CUP FINALS WERE THE FIRST TO BE TELEVISED IN COLOUR

DER KAISER FRANZ BECKENBAUER DAMAGED A CLAVICLE IN EXTRA TIME IN WEST GERMANY'S SEMI-FINAL WITH ITALY AND PLAYED THE REST OF THE MATCH WITH HIS ARM IN A SLING

PELE TRIES A SHOT FROM INSIDE HIS OWN HALF AGAINST CZECHOSLOVAKIA BUT THE BALL FLASHES NARROWLY WIDE

PELE FOOLS URUGUAYAN GOALKEEPER LADISLAO MAZURKIEWICZ WITH AN OUTRAGEOUS DUMMY BUT SHOT WIDE OF THE EMPTY NET

PELE'S SUBLIME STRIKE AGAINST THE CZECHS WHICH HAD ECHOES OF HIS GOAL IN THE 1958 FINAL

BRAZIL WORLD CUP WINNERS 1970. (FROM LEFT) CARLOS ALBERTO, BRITO,

GERSON, PIAZZA, EVERALDO, TOSTAO, CLODOALDO, RIVELINO, PELE, JAIRZINHO, FELIX

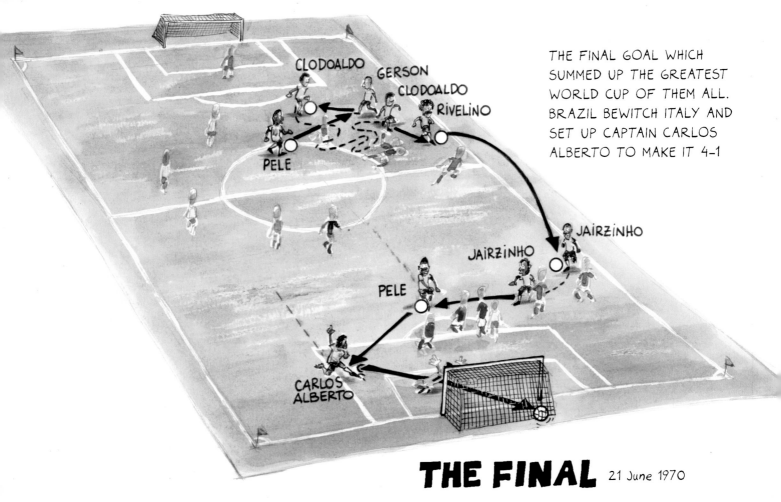

CLODOALDO
GERSON
CLODOALDO
RIVELINO

PELE

THE FINAL GOAL WHICH
SUMMED UP THE GREATEST
WORLD CUP OF THEM ALL.
BRAZIL BEWITCH ITALY AND
SET UP CAPTAIN CARLOS
ALBERTO TO MAKE IT 4-1

JAIRZINHO

JAIRZINHO

PELE

CARLOS
ALBERTO

THE FINAL 21 June 1970

BRAZIL 4 - 1 ITALY

Estadio Azteca, Mexico City
Attendance: 107,412
Referee: Rudi Glockner (East Germany)

FÉLIX
1

CARLOS ALBERTO   BRITO   PIAZZA   EVERALDO
4   2   3   16

CLODOALDO   GERSON
5   8

JAIRZINHO   TOSTÃO   PELÉ   RIVELINO
7   19   10   11

RIVA   BONINSEGNA   DOMENGHINI
11   20   13

DE SISTI   MAZZOLA   BERTINI
16   15   10

FACCHETTI   ROSATO   CERA   BURGNICH
3   8   5   2

ALBERTOSI
1

BRAZILIAN COACH MARIO ZAGALLO WAS
THE FIRST MAN TO WIN THE WORLD
CUP AS A PLAYER (1958 AND 1962) AND
COACH. HE TOOK OVER FROM JOAO
SALDANHA WHO WAS SACKED

1-0 PELE HEADS HOME

1-1 BONINSEGNA

2-1 GERSON SCORES FROM ABOUT 20 YARDS

3-1 JAIRZINHO

4-1 CARLOS ALBERTO SCORES AFTER PELE'S PASS

BRAZIL ARE THE WORLD CUP WINNERS AND PELE IS THE KING OF THE WORLD

Pele

ACZEL

1974 WEST GERMANY

GERD MULLER'S GOAL IN THE FINAL WAS HIS
14TH IN WORLD CUP FINALS

WITH BRAZIL KEEPING
THE JULES RIMET
TROPHY AFTER WINNING
IT FOR A THIRD TIME,
1974 SAW THE
INTRODUCTION OF A
NEW CUP

1974 W GERMANY

MOVE OVER, BRAZIL. In 1974 there was a new super-team ready to take over the world: the Netherlands, purveyors of total football, driven by Johann Cruyff, who'd accepted Pele's mantle as the world's best player.

Except that Holland, like Hungary 20 years earlier, didn't win. They came up against the hosts, as efficient as always, and lost in a thrilling final.

The Dutch had other players than Cruyff, of course. Ajax of Amsterdam had won the European Cup in 1971, '72 and '73 and the Dutch team for the final contained four of their players; by now the leading man had joined Barcelona. The Germans were not just about precision and power. They were led by 'Der Kaiser', Franz Beckenbauer, playing in his third World Cup finals and his second final. The deadly Gerd Müller again led the attack.

The reigning champions Brazil still had Jairzinho and Rivelinho but chose to fight and foul their way through the rounds while England and the USSR were missing.

East Germany were in the finals for the first time and they made a huge impact in the early rounds when they beat their neighbours West Germany and thus finished above the hosts in the group.

The cynics and conspiracy theorists noticed that by finishing second the West Germans avoided the Netherlands, Argentina and Brazil in the second stage. Instead they beat Yugoslavia and Sweden before winning the final pool match against Poland.

Come the final and the Dutch were overwhelming favourites. It began in sensational fashion when Holland went in front before the Germans had touched the ball. English referee Jack Taylor gave a penalty when Uli Hoeness tripped Cruyff after he ran from the centre circle following a move in which the Dutch passed the ball 13 times. It was the first penalty in a World Cup final and Johan Neeskens converted it.

The Germans equalised with a penalty of their own after 25 minutes – you wait 44 years for one penalty and then two come along at once! Paul Breitner scored it and West Germany began to get on top. Their second goal came from the remarkable Müller two minutes before half-time. It was his 68th goal in his 62nd and last international.

FRANZ BECKENBAUER HOLDS ALOFT THE NEW CUP, A SOLID-GOLD STATUETTE, WHICH SIGNALLED THE BEGINNING OF A NEW ERA

WEST GERMANY
FACED POLAND IN THE
SECOND GROUP PHASE
DESPITE THE RAIN
THAT SATURATED THE
FRANKFURT PITCH

POLAND'S GRZEGORZ
LATO WON THE GOLDEN
SHOE WITH SEVEN GOALS

OOPS... JUST BEFORE THE FINAL,
OFFICIALS DISCOVERED THE
CORNER FLAGS AND CENTRE-LINE
POSTS WERE MISSING!

THE WORLD CUP THROWS UP SOME ODD MOMENTS AND NONE
ODDER - OR FUNNIER - THAN WHEN MWEPU OF ZAIRE RAN
OUT OF THE DEFENSIVE WALL TO BOOT THE BALL AWAY
BEFORE BRAZIL HAD EVEN TAKEN THE FREE KICK

THE 1974 WORLD CUP WILL ALSO BE REMEMBERED FOR ITS HAIRSTYLES

JAN JONGBLOED

JOHAN NEESKENS

HANS-GEORG SCHWARZENBECK

WIM SUURBIER

PAUL BREITNER

GUNTER NETZER

JURGEN SPARWASSER SCORES THE GOAL FOR EAST GERMANY THAT WON THEIR MATCH WITH WEST GERMANY. BUT THE CONSPIRACY THEORISTS NOTED IT MEANT WEST GERMANY HAD THE EASIER SECOND ROUND

THE MAGESTIC JOHANN CRUYFF, THE DUTCH MASTER WAS INDISPUTABLY THE WORLD'S GREATEST PLAYER IN 1974 BUT HE WAS NEVER TO WIN A WORLD CUP WINNER'S MEDAL

THE DUTCH BEAT ARGENTINA 4-0 IN THE SECOND GROUP PHASE AND CRUYFF'S FIRST GOAL
WHICH OPENED THE SCORING WAS A CLASSIC

THE CRUYFF TURN

CRUYFF'S BRILLIANT VOLLEY AGAINST BRAZIL

WEST GERMANY WORLD CUP WINNERS 1974. (LEFT TO RIGHT) FRANZ BECKENBAUER, SEPP MAIER, HANS-GEORG SCHWARZENBECK, RAINER BONHOF, BERND HOLZENBEIN, JÜRGEN GRABOWSKI

GERD MULLER, WOLFGANG OVERATH, BERTI VOGTS, PAUL BREITNER, ULI HOENESS

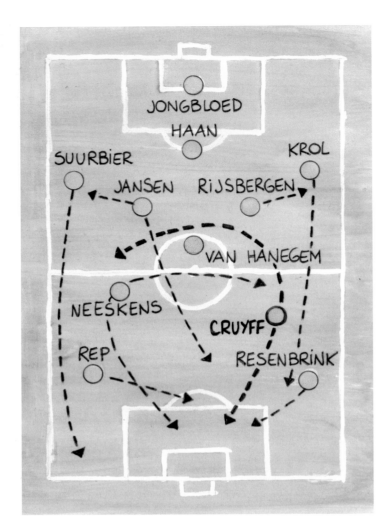

JONGBLOED
HAAN
SUURBIER
KROL
JANSEN   RIJSBERGEN
VAN HANEGEM
NEESKENS
CRUYFF
REP
RESENBRINK

(LEFT) THE DUTCH PLAYED "TOTAL FOOTBALL" WHICH MEANT EVERYONE COULD PLAY EVERYWHERE

(RIGHT) GERD MULLER CELEBRATES HIS WINNING GOAL IN THE FINAL, THE LAST AND 62ND GOAL FROM A 68 GAME INTERNATIONAL CAREER

THE FINAL 7 July 1974

NETHERLANDS 1- 2 W GERMANY

Olympiastadion, Munich
Attendance: 75,200
Referee: Jack Taylor (England)

MAIER
1
VOGTS
2
BECKENBAUER
5
BREITNER
3
SCHWARZENBECK
4
BONHOF
16
HOENESS
14
OVERATH
12
GRABOWSKI
6
MÜLLER
13
HÖLZENBEIN
17
RENSENBRINK
15
CRUYFF
14
REP
16
VAN HANEGEM
3
NEESKENS
13
JANSEN
6
RIJSBERGEN
17
KROL
12
HAAN
2
SUURBIER
20
JONGBLOED
8

WEST GERMAN COACH HELMUT SCHON, THE "LONG ONE". HE WAS 6FT 6INS TALL

TWO LEGENDS, JOHANN CRUYFF AND FRANZ BECKENBAUER, SHAKE HANDS BEFORE THE KICK-OFF

1st minute

HOENESS FOULS CRUYFF— PENALTY!

0-1 JOHANN NEESKENS

25th minute   HOLZENBEIN FOULED—PENALTY!

1-1 PAUL BREITNER

2-1

"DER BOMBER" TURNS AND SHOOTS AND STRIKES AGAIN TO WIN THE MATCH

GERMANY ARE WORLD CHAMPIONS

44th minute

1978 ARGENTINA

THE PAPER STORM.
THE 1978 WORLD CUP WAS NOTABLE
FOR THE STREAMS OF TORN UP
PAPER THAT CASCADED DOWN FROM
THE STANDS

1978 ARGENTINA

THE NETHERLANDS WERE READY to try again four years later but this time they travelled to South America without their talisman, Johann Cruyff. He had retired from international football the year before, claiming he did not want to play in Argentina because of the military dictatorship. In 2008 he revealed that the real reason was because his family were involved in a kidnap attempt.

Argentina had lost in the 1930 World Cup final in Uruguay; now on their own soil they were to go one better.

There was a first when Tunisia became the first African country to notch a victory at the World Cup finals. They beat Mexico 3-1 while fellow newcomers Iran drew with Scotland, the only British representatives. The Scots recovered to beat Holland 3-2 in their final group fixture but the two Dutch goals were enough to put them through on goal difference and Scotland went home, their campaign marred by a failed dope test by winger Willie Johnston.

Argentina's dubious 6-0 victory over Peru helped them top their group while Austria's 3-2 win put out neighbours and reigning champions West Germany as the Netherlands reached the final.

The feeling that the Argentines were using every possible method to assure a home victory strengthened when before the final the kick-off was delayed. Argentina kept the Dutch waiting and then captain Daniel Passarella objected to a plaster cast worn by René van de Kerkhof. The Dutch considered he was attempting to whip up hysteria in the crowd; not that he needed to: the fans were in a state of high excitement anyway. Perhaps surprisingly, Argentina won the fair play trophy as well as the cup itself.

In many ways the Dutch could be considered unlucky. Substitute Dirk Nanninga equalised a first-half goal by Mario Kempes and then Rob Rensenbrink hit the post in the dying seconds of normal time. The game went into extra time and Kempes and Daniel Bertoni gave their team football's ultimate prize.

It is difficult to argue against Argentina's right to the trophy. Some of their football was breathtaking. Kempes, the only foreign-based player in the squad, and Luque were often irresistible and behind them Osvaldo Ardiles, later to become a legend at Tottenham Hotspur, ensured a constant supply of opportunities.

MARIO KEMPES, "EL MATADOR", CELEBRATES HIS
GOAL IN THE FINAL AGAINST THE NETHERLANDS AND
GALVANISES THE WHOLE OF ARGENTINA. IT WAS
ONE OF SIX WHICH EARNED HIM THE GOLDEN SHOE

ARCHIE GEMMILL

ARCHIE GEMMILL'S GOAL
FOR SCOTLAND AGAINST
THE NETHERLANDS WENT
SOME WAY TO MAKING UP
FOR A MISERABLE WORLD
CUP FOR SCOTLAND

WORLD CUP GOAL NUMBER
1000

THE PENALTY SCORED BY ROB
RENSENBRINK, OF THE NETHERLANDS,
AGAINST SCOTLAND WAS THE 1000TH
GOAL SCORED IN THE COMPETITION

WELSH REFEREE CLIVE THOMAS TOOK THE LETTER OF THE LAW
TO A RIDICULOUS DEGREE WHEN OFFICIATING IN BRAZIL'S MATCH
AGAINST SWEDEN. HE RULED OUT A GOAL FROM ZICO WHICH WOULD
HAVE WON THE MATCH, SAYING HE HAD BLOWN FOR FULL TIME WHEN
THE BALL WAS IN THE AIR FOLLOWING A CORNER

THE 1978 WORLD CUP WAS THE ONLY
TIME A NATIONAL TEAM DID NOT WEAR
ITS OFFICIAL KIT. FRANCE'S KIT LOOKED
EXACTLY THE SAME AS HUNGARY'S ON
ARGENTINA'S BLACK AND WHITE TELEVISION
SYSTEM. SO FRANCE BORROWED A STRIP
FROM MAR DEL PLATA CLUB, ATLETICO
KIMBERLEY

ARGENTINA'S COACH CESAR LUIS MENOTTI
UPSET A 17-YEAR-OLD DIEGO MARADONA
BY LEAVING THE TEENAGER OUT OF THE
FINAL SQUAD OF 22 PLAYERS

ARIE HAAN'S SPECTACULAR 30-YARD SHOT WHICH LEFT DINO ZOFF FLOUNDERING AND PUT THE NETHERLANDS INTO THE FINAL INSTEAD OF ITALY

ZOFF WAS ALSO FLABBERGASTED BY NELINHO'S FABULOUS CURVING SHOT WHICH WON BRAZIL THE THIRD PLACE PLAY-OFF

DANIEL PASSARELLA, ARGENTINA'S CAPTAIN, HOLDS THE WORLD CUP ALOFT
AS A NATION WENT BANANAS

ARGENTINA WORLD CUP WINNERS 1978. (BACK ROW, LEFT TO RIGHT) DANIEL PASSARELLA, DANIEL BERTONI, JORGE OLGUIN, ALBERTO TARANTINI, MARIO KEMPES, UBALDO FILLOL

(FRONT) AMERICO GALLEGO, OSSIE ARDILES, LEOPOLDO LUQUE, OSCAR ORTIZ, LUIS GALVAN

ARGENTINA 6-0 PERU

TO GET TO THE FINAL ARGENTINA
NEEDED TO BEAT PERU 4-0.
THEY WON 6-0 AND IT DID NOT
GO UNNOTICED THAT PERU'S
GOALKEEPER RAMON QUIROGA
WAS AN ARGENTINIAN BORN IN
ROSARIO, THE TOWN IN WHICH THE
MATCH TOOK PLACE!

THE FINAL 25 June 1978

NETHERLANDS 1 - 3 (a.e.t) ARGENTINA

Estadio Monumental Antonio Vespucio Liberti,
Buenos Aires
Attendance: 71,483
Referee: Sergio Gonella (Italy)

FILLOL 5

OLGUÍN 15   GALVÁN 7   PASSARELLA 19   TARANTINI 20

ARDÍLES 2   GALLEGO 6   ORTÍZ 16   BERTONI 4

LUQUE 14   KEMPES 10

RENSENBRINK 12   REP 16

VAN DE KERKHOF R 10   VAN DE KERKHOF W 11   HAAN 9   NEESKENS 13

JANSEN 6   BRANDTS 22   KROL 5   POORTVLIET 2

JONGBLOED 8

THE CHAIN-SMOKING ARGENTINIAN COACH
CESAR LUIS MENOTTI ('EL FLACO' - THE
SKINNY ONE) MIXED SOUTH AMERICAN FLAIR
WITH EUROPEAN DISCIPLINE

1-0 KEMPES FORCES HIS WAY THROUGH THE DUTCH DEFENCE TO SWEEP THE BALL INTO THE NET FOR ARGENTINA'S OPENING GOAL!

37th minute

1-1 NANNINGA HEADS THE DUTCH LEVEL

81st minute

90th minute RENSENBRINK HITS THE POST

EXTRA-TIME

2-1

KEMPES!

105th minute

3-1 BERTONI SCORES AFTER A 1-2 WITH KEMPES

115th minute

ACZEL

1982 SPAIN

ITALY WON THE WORLD CUP FOR THE THIRD TIME WITH MARCO TARDELLI SCORING THEIR SECOND IN A 3-1 VICTORY OVER WEST GERMANY TO PROVIDE THE WORLD WITH ONE OF THE ALL-TIME GREAT CELEBRATIONS

1982 SPAIN

TWELVE YEARS ON FROM THE BRAZILIAN MASTERCLASS, the country that turned the game into an art form had produced another wonderful side. But they got only to the second group stage thanks to their own profligacy. Many fans considered they would have been worthy champions but this was Europe and pragmatism was king.

The Brazilians were beaten by Italy, who went on to become world champions for the third time. They were worthy winners although leading scorer Paolo Rossi took his time to get going. He failed to score as the Italians got through to the second round only by virtue of having scored just one more goal than Cameroon. But he then exploded with a hat-trick against Brazil and two more goals in the semi-final victory over Poland.

Italy also had 18-year-old full-back Giuseppe Bergomi, and while he became the youngest Italian to appear in the tournament, Northern Ireland's Norman Whiteside beat Pelé's record as the youngest player in the competition's history. He was just 17 years and 41 days old.

He helped provide one of the main surprises of the first round, Northern Ireland beating Spain 1-0 to reach the second stage.

Had Brazil possessed a goalscorer to match Romario and Ronaldo, who were still to come, they would surely have swept all before them. Their midfield of Zico, Falcão, Socrates, Cerezo and Éder produced some fluid and fashionable football.

They extracted revenge for 1978 with a 3-1 victory over Argentina in the second phase. Maradona, now arguably the world's greatest player, was sent off for kicking Batista and Brazil needed just a draw against Italy to go through to the semi-finals. But despite goals from Socrates and Falcão, Rossi's hat-trick sent them home.

The Italians faced Poland in the Camp Nou in their semi and a goal in each half from Rossi ensured a place in the final. In the meantime in Seville, the West Germans were facing France in a match made infamous by goalkeeper Harald Schumacher's assault on the French substitute Patrick Battiston. The German goalkeeper was not even booked by Dutch referee Charles Corver, who gave a goal-kick. The Germans went through from the World Cup finals' first penalty shoot-out.

Their exertions undoubtedly played a part in the final. West Germany were always second best. Italy could even afford to ignore a penalty miss by Antonio Cabrini.

LIFE BEGINS AT 40! DINO ZOFF GAVE HOPE TO MILLIONS OF MEN BY CAPTAINING ITALY
EVEN THOUGH HE'D CELEBRATED HIS 40TH BIRTHDAY THE PREVIOUS FEBRUARY

SHEIKH FAHID AL-AHMAD AL-SABAH, PRESIDENT OF THE KUWAITI FOOTBALL ASSOCIATION, LEADS HIS COUNTRY'S PROTESTS AFTER THE SOVIET REFEREE MIROSLAV STUPAR AWARDS A DISPUTED GOAL TO FRANCE. THE REF CHANGED HIS MIND

A GREAT GOAL FROM BELLOUMI HELPS ALGERIA TO A SHOCK 2-1 VICTORY OVER WEST GERMANY IN GROUP 2

BUT THE GERMANS WENT THROUGH AFTER A FARCE OF A MATCH AGAINST AUSTRIA. THE GERMANS HAD TO WIN 1-0 TO GO THROUGH AND WITH THE AUSTRIANS HAVING ALREADY QUALIFIED THEY CONSPIRED IN A MEANINGLESS ENCOUNTER

BRAZIL WERE EVERYBODY'S FAVOURITES BUT COMPLACENT DEFENDING LET THEM DOWN.
HERE CEREZO GIVES THE BALL AWAY AND PAOLO ROSSI SCORES THE SECOND OF HIS
HAT-TRICK IN ITALY'S 3–2 WIN

ROSSI TOOK A WHILE TO WARM UP BUT HIS SIX GOALS IN THE TOURNAMENT EARNED HIM THE GOLDEN
SHOE. HE HAD RETURNED IN STYLE FROM A TWO-YEAR BAN FOR HIS PART IN A MATCH-FIXING
SCANDAL

IN THE SEMI-FINAL WEST
GERMAN GOALKEEPER
HARALD SCHUMACHER
CLATTERS INTO PATRICK
BATTISTON TO DENY THE
FRENCHMAN A GOAL-SCORING
OPPORTUNITY. PARAMEDICS
HAD TO ADMINISTER OXYGEN
AND MICHEL PLATINI SAID HE
THOUGHT HIS TEAM-MATE WAS
DEAD. SCHUMACHER ON BEING
TOLD BATTISTON HAD LOST
THREE TEETH SAID: "IF THAT'S
ALL THAT'S WRONG WITH HIM,
I'LL BUY HIM THE CROWNS."
ALL DUTCH REFEREE CHARLES
CORVER DID WAS GIVE A
GOALKICK!

ITALY WORLD CUP WINNERS 1982. (BACK ROW, LEFT TO RIGHT) DINO ZOFF, FRANCESCO GRAZIANI GIUSEPPE BERGOMI GAETANO SCIREA FULVIO COLLOVATI CLAUDIO GENTILE

(FRONT) BRUNO CONTI, PAOLO ROSSI, GABRIELE ORIALI, ANTONIO CABRINI,

FRENCH CAPTAIN MICHEL PLATINI WAS ONE OF THE WORLD'S GREAT PLAYERS BUT HIS INTERNATIONAL CAREER HIGHLIGHT WAS THE SEMI-FINAL DEFEAT BY WEST GERMANY

THE FINAL 11 July 1982

ITALY 3-1 WEST GERMANY

Estadio Santiago Bernabeu, Madrid
Attendance: 90,000
Referee: Arnaldo Czar Coelho (Brazil)

ENZO BEARZOT LED ITALY TO THEIR THIRD WORLD CUP TRIUMPH WITH A MOST UN-ITALIAN ATTACKING PHILOSOPHY

24th minute

BREIGEL FOULS CONTI - PENALTY!

BUT CABRINI MISSES

1-0 ROSSI HEADS HOME

57th minute

2-0 TARDELLI

69th minute

3-0 ALTOBELLI

82nd minute

3-1 BREITNER GETS A CONSOLATION GOAL

83rd minute

DIEGO
(10)

ACZEL

1986 MEXICO

DIEGO MARADONA WAS INSTRUMENTAL IN ARGENTINA'S SECOND WORLD CUP TRIUMPH BUT HE WAS A CONTROVERSIAL FIGURE

1986 MEXICO

THIS TOURNAMENT IS MOSTLY REMEMBERED for the man described by *L'Equipe*, the French sports newspaper, as 'half angel, half devil'. Diego Maradona, a god to many Argentines, but a genius remembered with something less than affection by many fans from other countries, especially England.

Mexico became the first country to stage the tournament for a second time. Despite the heat and altitude they were chosen after Colombia withdrew for financial reasons. And they staged the tournament despite a terrible earthquake less than a year before, which killed some 20,000 people.

The changing face of football was illustrated by the fact that Morocco topped England's group to become the first African team to reach the second round. England beat Paraguay and then came the fateful meeting with Argentina. Considering the history between the teams the quarter-final meeting at the Azteca Stadium was a classic but it seemed only the referee, Ali Bin Nasser of Tunisia, failed to spot Maradona's blatant handball for the first goal. FIFA were accused of allowing an inexperienced referee to officiate in a match that always had the potential to explode.

To England's credit they kept their cool, even after Maradona scored a second which must go down in history as one of the greatest ever World Cup goals. In 2002 it was voted 'the goal of the century' on the FIFA website. Villain and hero all in one game.

Scotland went home following a physical goalless draw with Uruguay. José Batista, of Uruguay, claimed an unwanted World Cup record that still stands when he was dismissed for a foul on Gordon Strachan after less than one minute of play.

France, the European champions, put out Brazil but fell 2-0 to West Germany in one semi-final while Argentina beat Belgium 2-0 in the other, Maradona scoring another goal to remember.

West Germany set Lothar Matthäus to mark Maradona in the final and Argentina's captain was not his usual ebullient self. It was down to the foot soldiers to put Argentina ahead only for the Germany to level at 2-2.

But Maradona was not to be denied his moment; he sent Jorge Burruchaga scampering away seven minutes from time and Argentina were able to win a second world crown in eight years.

ARGENTINA'S FIRST GOAL IN THEIR 2-1 DEFEAT OF ENGLAND WAS A CLEAR HANDBALL.
"THE HAND OF GOD" MARADONA CALLED IT. THE ENGLISH PREFERRED "THE HAND OF A CHEAT"

BUT MARADONA'S SECOND IN THE MATCH HAS BEEN CALLED "THE GOAL OF THE CENTURY".
THE NO. 10 PICKED UP THE BALL IN HIS OWN HALF, BEAT PETER BEARDSLEY AND PETER REID, AND
DASHED TOWARD'S ENGLAND'S GOAL. THE CROWD IN THE AZTECA STADIUM HELD ITS COLLECTIVE

BREATH AS HE WENT PAST TERRY BUTCHER AND THEN TERRY FENWICK BEFORE ROUNDING PETER SHILTON AND SLOTTING THE BALL INTO THE NET. EVEN THEN ENGLAND RALLIED AND SCORED THROUGH GARY LINEKER WHO ALMOST EQUALISED

GARY LINEKER, OF ENGLAND, ENDED THE
TOURNAMENT WITH THE GOLDEN SHOE,
SCORING SIX TIMES

A FEATURE OF THE TOURNAMENT WAS THE
"MEXICAN WAVE", AN IRRITATING CROWD HABIT
WHICH HAS BEDEVILLED SPORTS EVENTS EVER
SINCE

ON HIS 31ST BIRTHDAY, MICHEL PLATINI KISSES
THE BALL BEFORE TAKING HIS PENALTY IN THE
QUARTER-FINAL SHOOT-OUT AGAINST BRAZIL.
WHATEVER FORCES THE KISS WAS DESIGNED TO
INVOKE DID NOT COME TO HIS AID. HIS SPOT
KICK FLEW OVER THE BAR. BUT FRANCE WON
THE SHOOT-OUT 4-3 AND FRANCE WENT ON TO
LOSE TO WEST GERMANY IN THE SEMIS FOR THE
SECOND SUCCESSIVE TIME

ARGENTINA WORLD CUP WINNERS 1986. (BACK ROW, LEFT TO RIGHT) SERGIO BATISTA,
JOSE CUCIUFFO, JULIO OLARTICOECHEA, NERY PUMPIDO, JOSE BROWN, OSCAR RUGGERI,

(FRONT) JORGE BURRUCHAGA, RICARDO GIUSTI, HECTOR ENRIQUE,

MARADONA ALSO SCORED AGAINST BELGIUM AFTER A SOLO RUN

CARLOS BILARDO, THE ARGENTINIAN COACH, WAS HEAVILY CRITICISED FOR HIS DEFENSIVE TACTICS. BUT EVERYONE BEGGED FORGIVENESS AFTER HIS TEAM'S TRIUMPH

THE FINAL 29 June 1986

ARGENTINA 3 - 2 WEST GERMANY

Estadio Azteca, Mexico City
Attendance: 114,600
Referee: Romualdo Arppi Filho (Brazil)

1-0 SCHUMACHER BOOBS AND BROWN HEADS HOME

23rd minute

2-0 VALDANO

55th minute

2-1 RUMMENIGGE STRETCHES TO SCORE

74th minute

2-2 VOLLER LEVELS

82nd minute

3-2 A DREAM PASS FROM MARADONA GIVES BURRUCHAGA THE CHANCE TO SCORE THE WINNER

85th minute

ACZEL

90th minute

MARADONA DIVES BUT NO PENALTY

ARGENTINA AND MARADONA ARE THE WORLD CHAMPIONS

CHUICK!

1990 ITALY

WEST GERMANY GET THEIR OWN BACK ON ARGENTINA FOR THE 1986 DEFEAT, ANDREAS BREHME SCORED THE ONLY GOAL OF A POOR FINAL FROM THE PENALTY SPOT

1990 ITALY

IN ENGLAND this is remembered as the tournament of Gazza's tears, when the English middle class was attracted to football. They've been trying to elbow out the working-class supporter ever since.

Paul Gascoigne was booked in the quarter-final and cried when he realised he'd miss the final if England won. They didn't. West Germany beat them in a penalty shoot-out and went on to avenge their defeat by Argentina four years earlier. Their victory was a triumph for Franz Beckenbauer, who emulated Mario Zagallo, the first man to win the World Cup as a player and a coach.

It was not a great tournament in terms of goals, being the lowest-scoring with just 2.21 per game, but there was excitement and drama aplenty, especially in the opening match when Cameroon beat Argentina at the San Siro.

Cameroon's progress to the quarter-finals provided the biggest romance and in Roger Milla, they had a genuine star.

After coming off the bench against Romania, he scored the two goals that took the Indomitable Lions into the second round. He repeated the feat against Colombia — celebrating by dancing with the corner flag — and Africa had its first quarter-finalists. It was only two Gary Lineker penalties that took England through in a quarter-final in which Cameroon led 2-1 with ten minutes to go.

Italy reached the semi-finals as well, thanks to a great goal from Roberto Baggio against Czechoslovakia and a World Cup record for goalkeeper Walter Zenga. He kept five clean sheets and went 517 minutes unbeaten. However, they ran up against Diego Maradona at his old stamping ground in Naples and went out.

The locals were split, half supporting Maradona, the others going with Italy. But the Argentinian hero was not the podgy no. 10. It was goalkeeper Sergio Goycochea, who had come in after Nery Pumpido broke a leg in the second match. Goycochea saved two penalties in the shoot-out to put Argentina into the final after a 1-1 draw.

There was no repeat in the Rome final, Andreas Brehme's penalty winning a poor match. There were two firsts for Argentina. They became the first team not to score in the final — it did not help that Claudio Caniggia was suspended — and the first to have a man sent off: Pedro Monzón. Another of the team, Gustavo Dezotti, also went.

ROGER MILLA OF CAMEROON WAS A COLOURFUL PRESENCE IN A GENERALLY DRAB
WORLD CUP WITH HIS TRADEMARK GOAL CELEBRATION. HE WAS PERSUADED OUT OF
RETIREMENT AT THE AGE OF 38

OMAM BIYIK SCORED THE GOAL THAT GAVE CAMEROON A SHOCK 1-0 VICTORY OVER THE REIGNING CHAMPIONS ARGENTINA EVEN THOUGH THE AFRICANS FINISHED WITH NINE MEN

COLOMBIAN GOALKEEPER RENE HIGUITA GIFTED CAMEROON A GOAL IN THE SECOND ROUND BY TRYING TO DRIBBLE AROUND ROGER MILLA. IT MEANT CAMEROON WERE THE FIRST AFRICAN COUNTRY TO REACH THE QUARTER-FINALS

ITALY'S ROBERTO BAGGIO SCORED
THE GREATEST GOAL OF THE 1990
TOURNAMENT WITH A DASH THROUGH
THE CZECHOSLOVAK DEFENCE

WEST GERMAN CAPTAIN LOTHAR MATTHAUS
SCORED TWICE AGAINST YUGOSLAVIA
AND LED WEST GERMANY TO THEIR THIRD TITLE

AN UGLY ASPECT OF THE 1990 WORLD CUP WAS THE DISGRACEFUL BEHAVIOUR OF FRANK RIJKAARD OF HOLLAND WHO SPAT AT GERMANY'S RUDI VOLLER. BOTH WERE SENT OFF

TOTO SCHILLACI (RIGHT), WHO WON THE GOLDEN SHOE WITH SIX GOALS, COULDN'T UNDERSTAND WHY HE WAS FREQUENTLY GIVEN OFFSIDE IN THE SEMI-FINAL

CLAUDIO CANIGGIA EQUALISES FOR ARGENTINA IN THEIR SEMI-FINAL IN NAPLES AND ARGENTINA GO ON TO WIN ON PENALTIES

WEST GERMANY WORLD CUP WINNERS 1990. (BACK ROW, LEFT TO RIGHT) OSIECK (ASSISTANT COACH), FRANZ BECKENBAUER (COACH), KLAUS AUGENTHALER, STEFAN REUTER, JURGEN KLINSMANN, FRANK MILL, GUIDO BUCHWALD, PAUL STEINER, THOMAS BERTHOLD, ANDREAS KOPKE, JURGEN KOHLER, ANDREAS MOLLER, HANS PFLUGLER, BERTI VOGTS (ASSISTANT COACH)

(FRONT) PIERRE LITTBARSKI, THON (GOALKEEPER COACH), ANDREAS BREHME,
LOTHAR MATTHAUS, KARLHEINZ RIEDLE, BODO ILLNGER, UWE BEIN, GUNTHER HERMANN,
RUDI VOLLER, THOMAS HASSLER, RAIMOND AUMANN

IN ENGLAND THE WORLD CUP WAS KNOWN FOR GAZZA'S TEARS. GAZZA, AKA PAUL GASCOIGNE, ENGLAND'S CHARISMATIC, IF OCCASIONALLY MANIC, PLAY-MAKER, CRIED IN THE SEMI-FINAL WITH WEST GERMANY WHEN HE REALISED THAT TWO BOOKINGS WOULD EXCLUDE HIM FROM THE FINAL SHOULD ENGLAND WIN. THEY DIDN'T BUT GAZZA ENCHANTED A NATION FED UP WITH LOSING TO THE GERMANS!

FRANZ BECKENBAUER COACHED WEST GERMANY TO SUCCESS, THUS BECOMING ONLY THE SECOND MAN TO WIN THE WORLD CUP AS A PLAYER AND COACH. THE FIRST WAS BRAZIL'S MARIO ZAGALLO

THE FINAL 8 July 1990

WEST GERMANY 1 - 0 ARGENTINA

Stadio Olimpico, Rome
Attendance: 73,603
Referee: Edgardo Codesal Mendez (Mexico)

65th minute

MONZON SENT OFF AFTER CHOPPING DOWN KLINSMANN, WHO SOME SAY DIVED

85th minute PENALTY!

VOLLER IS BROUGHT DOWN. AGAIN THERE WERE SUGGESTIONS OF A DIVE

1-0 GOYCOCHEA GOES THE RIGHT WAY BUT BREHME'S PENALTY IS TOO GOOD

GOAL!!! AND HIS TEAM-MATES MOB VOLLER

RED FOR DEZOTTI AFTER FOUL ON VOLLER

87th minute

THE FINAL WHISTLE

MATTHAUS CONSOLES MARADONA

BUT HE JOINS HIS TEAM-MATES AS THEY CELEBRATE WINNING AGAIN AFTER TWO SUCCESSIVE LOSING FINALS

1994 USA

ROBERTO BAGGIO HANGS HIS HEAD AFTER MISSING THE PENALTY IN THE FINAL'S SHOOT-OUT WHICH GIFTED THE TROPHY TO BRAZIL. GOALKEEPER TAFFAREL CANNOT BELIEVE IT

1994 USA

THIS WAS THE FIRST TIME the World Cup finals had been held outside of South America or Europe. Indeed, the tournament was staged in a country in which football was not a major sport. It might have been expected that football in the US would have kicked on after the 1-0 success over England in 1950 but the reasoning in America was that it couldn't be much of a sport if a team of part-timers could beat a team reckoned to be among the favourites.

But FIFA President João Havelange wanted to spread football's message and in one way it proved the correct decision. The tournament attracted 3,587,538 spectators, the most at any finals, at an average of nearly 70,000 a match.

It was, though, won by a familiar name. Brazil gained the cup for the fourth time, although theirs was not a vintage team.

There were shocks. Bulgaria, who had never won a World Cup match in 16 attempts, put out West Germany on their way to the semi-finals and Romania, inspired by Gheorghe Hagi, beat the Maradona-less Argentina. The Republic of Ireland, still managed by Jack Charlton, an England hero of 1966, qualified while other European teams such as England and France did not and a goal from Ray Houghton meant the Irish beat Italy 1-0.

But the Italians sneaked into the Round of 16 by being one of the best third-placed teams.

Sadly for Cameroon their Lions were not so indomitable this time. They managed only one point when finishing bottom of their group but Roger Milla's goal against Russia meant he broke his own record as the World Cup's oldest scorer – at 42 years, one month and eight days.

Brazil had a fabulous cutting edge in the mercurial Romario and his sidekick Bebeto. But the rest of the Brazilian side was prosaic. No longer did they contain a fabulous winger, or even midfielders who ran past their forwards, or even, as later, full-backs who reached the byline, The side's style was summed up in their captain, the defensive midfielder Dunga.

Brazil v Italy looked on paper the perfect final. Two countries, each of whom had won the competition three times, coming together to make World Cup history. But it was a dull affair, the first to be decided by a penalty shoot-out.

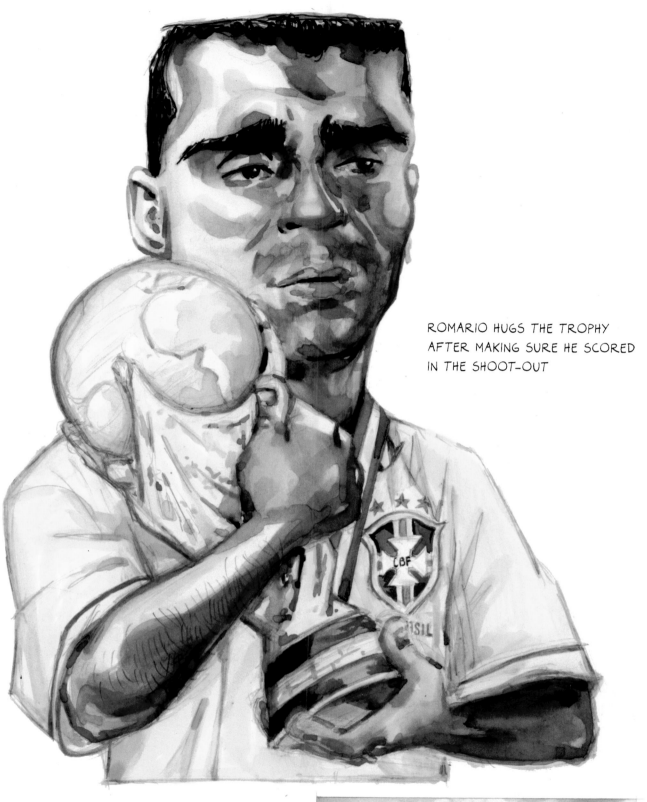

ROMARIO HUGS THE TROPHY
AFTER MAKING SURE HE SCORED
IN THE SHOOT-OUT

A FAMOUS WORLD CUP CELEBRATION,.
BEBETO (CENTRE) CELEBRATES SCORING
IN THE QUARTER-FINAL WITH HOLLAND BY
PRETENDING TO ROCK THE BABY BORN TO HIS
WIFE DAYS BEFORE THE MATCH. MAZINHO AND
ROMARIO JOIN IN

THE OPENING CEREMONY SHOWED WHAT
FOOTBALL MEANT TO THE USA. SINGER DIANA
ROSS'S FEEBLE PENALTY ATTEMPT GOES WIDE

THE BULGARIAN MATCH WITH MEXICO IN THE FIRST KNOCK-
OUT STAGE WAS SO BORING THAT EVEN THE GOALPOSTS
GAVE UP AND HAD TO BE REPLACED

MARADONA WOULD
HAVE BEEN PROUD
OF SAEED AL
OWAIRAN'S GOAL
AGAINST BELGIUM

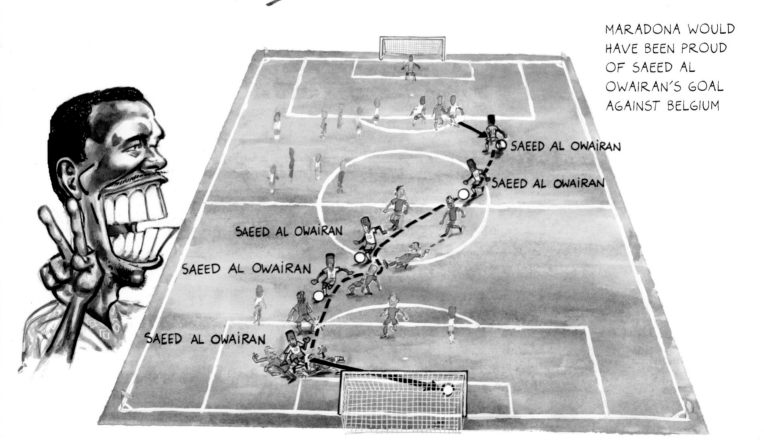

HRISTO STOICHKOV, STAR OF THE
BULGARIAN TEAM WHICH REACHED
THE SEMI-FINALS FOR THE FIRST
TIME, AND OLEG SALENKO OF
RUSSIA SHARED THE GOLDEN SHOE
WITH SIX GOALS APIECE. SALENKO
SCORED FIVE OF HIS IN THE
GROUP MATCH WITH CAMEROON,
A WORLD CUP RECORD. IN THAT
MATCH ROGER MILLA SCORED FOR
CAMEROON, AT 42 THE OLDEST
PLAYER TO APPEAR IN THE WORLD
CUP FINALS

MARADONA'S CONTROVERSIAL WORLD
CUP CAREER ENDS WHEN THE GREAT NO. 10
FAILED A DRUG TEST AND WAS SENT HOME

COLOMBIAN ANDRES ESCOBAR'S OWN GOAL IN
THEIR 2-1 FIRST ROUND DEFEAT BY THE USA
HAD TRAGIC CONSEQUENCES. COLOMBIA WENT
HOME AND ESCOBAR WAS SHOT TO DEATH TEN
DAYS AFTER THE GAME

YORDAN LETCHKOV HEADED THE WINNING
GOAL FOR BULGARIA IN THEIR 2-1
QUARTER-FINAL DEFEAT OF REIGNING
CHAMPIONS WEST GERMANY

LEONARDO OF BRAZIL, GENERALLY RECOGNISED AS ONE OF FOOTBALL'S GENTLEMEN, WAS SENT OFF FOR ELBOWING TAB RAMOS OF THE USA. HE WAS SUSPENDED FOR THE REST OF THE TOURNAMENT

BRAZIL WORLD CUP WINNERS 1994 (BACK ROW, LEFT TO RIGHT) TAFFAREL, JORGINHO, ALDAIR, MAURO SILVA, MARCIO SANTOS, BRANCO

(FRONT) MAZINHO, ROMARIO, DUNGA, BEBETO, ZINHO

ROBERTO BAGGIO'S NICKNAME WAS
"THE DIVINE PONY TAIL". THE SECOND
PART WAS OBVIOUS BUT THE FIRST
CAME FROM HIS BUDDHIST RELIGION

CARLOS PARREIRA BROUGHT A NEW
PHILOSOPHY TO BRAZILIAN COACHING
SYSTEM WHEN HE TOOK OVER. INSTEAD OF
FLAMBOYANT ATTACK HE PREFERRED A
FUNCTIONAL DEFENCE

THE FINAL 10 July 1994

BRAZIL ⓪ - ⓪ (a.e.t) ITALY

Penalties 3-2

Rose Bowl, Pasadena
Attendance: 94,194
Referee: Sandor Puhl (Hungary)

FOUR
WORLD
CUPS

TAFFAREL
1

JORGINHO   ALDAIR   MARCIO SANTOS   BRANCO
2   13   15   6

MAZINHO   MAURO SILVA   DUNGA   ZINHO
17   5   8   9

BEBETO   ROMARIO
7   11

MASSARO   BAGGIO, R
19   10

DONADONI   ALBERTINI   BAGGIO, D   BERTI
16   11   13   14

BENARRIVO   MALDINI   BARESI   MUSSI
3   5   6   8

PAGLIUCA
1

85th minute

AFTER 120 BORING MINUTES...

...THE FIRST PENALTY SHOOT-OUT IN A WORLD CUP FINAL IS INEVITABLE

BARESI 0-0

MARCIO SANTOS 0-0
(PAGLIUCA SAVES)
ALBERTINI   0-1
ROMARIO   1-1
EVANI   1-2
BRANCO   2-2

MASSARO 2-2
(TAFFAREL SAVES)

DUNGA 3-2

BAGGIO PUTS THE BALL ON THE SPOT,...

...AND MISSES!

BRAZIL WORLD CHAMPIONS

ACZEL

1998 FRANCE

AN OUT-OF-SORTS RONALDO,
OF BRAZIL, COLLIDES WITH
FRENCH GOALKEEPER,
FABIEN BARTHEZ

1998 FRANCE

IT WAS ALWAYS A SHAME that France had never won the World Cup. Failure in 1938 and two semi-final defeats in the 1980s, both by West Germany, meant the country that gave the tournament to the world were always the bridesmaids.

But at home in 1998 they ended their run of failures with a swagger, winning a tournament that contained 32 teams for the first time. The critics said it was too bloated, but Les Bleus didn't care.

The Brazilians would quickly show they had cast off their dour image. Dunga was still there, beavering away in midfield, but full-backs Roberto Carlos and Cafu raced forward, Rivaldo was a creative presence and up front they had paired Bebeto with 21-year-old Ronaldo.

Was the Brazilian wonder boy the best player in the world, or was that Zinedine Zidane, a worthy heir to the great players who had worn the no. 10 shirt? It provoked many arguments among fans but what was indisputable was that the French team contained as many great players as Brazil. Lilian Thuram, at right-back, Laurent Blanc at centre-half, Didier Deschamps, the 'water carrier' in midfield, the quicksilver Youri Djorkaeff linking the attack. If only Thierry Henry had been a year or two older, because the one thing the French lacked was someone to lead their attack.

England had qualified this time with a so-called 'golden' generation. There was 18-year-old Michael Owen and 23-year-old David Beckham. But they were mugged by Romania in the group stages, which meant they faced old adversaries Argentina, runaway winners of group H. The game went into extra time and then a penalty shoot-out. England entrusted their final penalty to David Batty, the Leeds defensive midfielder, and Roa saved it.

France needed extra time and a golden goal (used in the tournament for the first time) from Blanc to beat Paraguay while in the quarter-final they got revenge on Italy for defeat in 1938.

France faced Croatia, the tournament's surprise package, in the semis. Playing in their first World Cup following the break-up of Yugoslavia, Croatia had beaten Germany 3-0 in the quarter-final but France squeezed through.

Penalties decided the other semi between Brazil and the Netherlands and it was another 'perfect' final – the first time the hosts had faced the reigning champions. But it was a day shrouded in mystery and intrigue over Ronaldo and Brazil were no match for France.

ZINEDINE ZIDANE, THE FRENCH PLAY-MAKER WHO FOLLOWED IN THE FOOTSTEPS OF PELE AND
MARADONA AND THE OTHER GREAT NO. 10s

CROATIA WERE IN THE FINALS FOR THE FIRST TIME AND THEIR STRIKER, DAVOR SUKER, TOOK HOME THE GOLDEN SHOE WITH SIX GOALS

AGAINST JAMAICA GABRIEL BATISTUTA, OF ARGENTINA, BECAME ONLY THE FOURTH PLAYER TO SCORE TWO WORLD CUP HAT-TRICKS AND THE FIRST TO SCORE HAT-TRICKS IN TWO WORLD CUPS

LAURENT BLANC SCORES THE FIRST GOLDEN GOAL IN THE WORLD CUP WHEN FRANCE BEAT PARAGUAY 1-0

LAURENT BLANC STARTED A SUPERSTITION WHEN, BEFORE EVERY MATCH,
HE KISSED THE BALD HEAD OF FRENCH GOALKEEPER FABIEN BARTHEZ. BUT ALTHOUGH
BLANC MISSED THE FINAL, SUSPENDED AFTER BEING SENT OFF FOLLOWING A
THEATRICAL REACTION FROM CROATIA'S SLAVEN BILIC, IT DIDN'T MATTER

OWEN'S GOAL

MICHAEL OWEN BURST INTO THE WORLD CUP AT 19 WITH A WONDER GOAL AGAINST ARGENTINA IN THE ROUND OF 16, EVOKING MEMORIES OF DIEGO MARADONA AND 1986. THE MATCH FINISHED 2-2 AND ARGENTINA WON THE PENALTY SHOOT-OUT

 DAVID BECKHAM THE HISTORY OF BAD FEELING BETWEEN ENGLAND AND ARGENTINA MANIFESTED ITSELF AGAIN WHEN DAVID BECKHAM REACTED TO BEING CHOPPED DOWN BY DIEGO SIMEONE BY FLICKING OUT A FOOT. SIMEONE REACTED AS IF HE'D BEEN SHOT AND BECKHAM WAS SENT OFF

HAVING BEATEN ENGLAND, ARGENTINA WENT OUT AT THE QUARTER-FINAL STAGE TO THE GOAL OF THE WORLD CUP SCORED BY DENNIS BERGKAMP OF THE NETHERLANDS

FRANCE WORLD CUP WINNERS 1998 (BACK ROW, LEFT TO RIGHT) ZINEDINE ZIDANE,
MARCEL DESAILLY FRANK LEBOEUF LILIAN THURAM STEPHANE GUIVARC'H EMMANUEL PETIT

(FRONT) CHRISTIAN KARAMBEU, YOURI DJORKAEFF, DIDIER DESCHAMPS,
FABIEN BARTHEZ, BIXENTE LIZARAZU

DEFENDER LILIAN THURAM
RESCUED FRANCE WITH
BOTH GOALS AFTER
THEY CAME FROM BEHIND
TO BEAT CROATIA 2-1
IN THE SEMI-FINALS.
THEY WERE HIS ONLY
INTERNATIONAL GOALS IN
142 APPEARANCES

THE CROWDS IN PARIS WERE A FEATURE
OF THE 1998 WORLD CUP

THE FINAL 12 July 1998

BRAZIL 0 - 3 FRANCE

Stade de France, Saint-Denis
Attendance: 75,000
Referee: Said Belqola (Morocco)

FRENCH COACH AIME JACQUET

WILL HE, WON'T HE? THE BRAZILIANS CHANGE
THEIR MIND ABOUT RONALDO.

1-0 ZIDANE HEADS HOME A CORNER

27th minute

2-0 ZIDANE'S HEAD AGAIN

45th minute

KISS!

A RED CARD FOR DESAILLY FOR A
FOUL ON CAFU

68th minute

3-0 PETIT

90th minute

FRANCE CHAMPIONS,
BRAZIL BEWILDERED

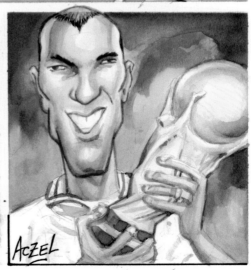

ACZEL

2002 S KOREA/JAPAN

RONALDO GETS HIS OWN BACK WITH A GLITTERING PERFORMANCE IN SOUTH KOREA TO GIVE BRAZIL THEIR FIFTH WORLD CUP

2002 S KOREA/JAPAN

THE FOOTBALL WORLD WAS CHANGING RAPIDLY. FIFA had decided that the World Cup finals could be shared between two countries with little history or tradition in the sport and the result was a tournament full of surprises and not a little controversy. Conspiracy theorists were handed a plate full of goodies.

But the old order prevailed. The final was played between Brazil and a lucky German side whose good fortune did not extend to the last match.

The suspicion that South Korea and Japan were chosen for marketing reasons – lots of shirts etc. to sell – never really went away but the shocks started in the very first match when Senegal, making their debut at this stage, beat the holders France 1-0 in Seoul. The French, still able to field most of the men who won the cup in 1998, did not recover, finishing bottom of Group A without scoring a single goal.

England were in what was described as 'the group of death' against Argentina (the computer that sorted the fixtures must have had a mischievous streak), Sweden and Nigeria. Argentina beat Nigeria but then, in the match the world was waiting to see, lost 1-0 to England. By a delicious irony the goal that settled it was scored from the penalty spot by David Beckham. A 1-1 draw with Sweden and Argentina were on their way home.

Korea, managed by Guus Hiddink, came from behind to beat Italy through Ahn Jung Hwan's golden goal but went out in the semis. Their co-hosts reached the round of 16 but were beaten by Turkey. Turkey had qualified from Brazil's group with just four points. But the Turks had legitimate cause for complaint in their 2-1 group defeat by Brazil. They led through a Hasan Sas goal, only for Ronaldo to equalise just after half-time. Then, as the game headed to a close, Alpay was sent off for his second bookable offence, which led to a penalty from Rivaldo even though the offence was clearly outside the penalty area. There were no histrionics in the semi-final, though, as a Ronaldo goal settled the issue.

Germany, meanwhile, staggered towards the final. They had won their group comfortably enough, thanks to an 8-0 victory over Saudi Arabia. But they then needed three unconvincing single-goal victories against three of the tournament's less distinguished teams – Paraguay, the USA and South Korea. They were no match for Ronaldo, compensating for the problems of four years earlier, in the final.

GERMANY'S FAMOUSLY IRASCIBLE OLIVER KAHN IS THE ONLY GOALKEEPER
TO WIN THE GOLDEN BALL FOR THE TOURNAMENT'S BEST PLAYER ALTHOUGH
IT WAS HIS MISTAKE IN THE FINAL THAT GIFTED THE CUP TO BRAZIL

DAVID BECKHAM GOT HIS OWN BACK AGAINST ARGENTINA AFTER HIS RED CARD FOUR YEARS PREVIOUSLY WHEN HE SCORED THE ONLY GOAL OF THE GROUP GAME, A DEFEAT WHICH CONTRIBUTED TO ARGENTINA'S FAILURE TO GET INTO THE SECOND ROUND

OH DEAR! RONALDINHO SHOUTS FOR JOY AS DAVID SEAMAN SCRAMBLES BACK IN VAIN TO STOP A FREE KICK FROM THE MERCURIAL BRAZILIAN FROM ENTERING HIS NET AND GIVING BRAZIL A 2-1 QUARTER-FINAL VICTORY

RIVALDO OF BRAZIL GETS HIT ON THE LEG BUT COLLAPSES HOLDING HIS FACE. TURKEY'S UNSAL WAS SENT OFF FOR A SECOND YELLOW CARD AS REFEREE KIM YOUNG JOO, OF KOREA, WAS FOOLED BY THE BRAZILIAN'S OVER-REACTION

WHEN THE TEAMS MET IN THE SEMI-FINAL A SIMPLE TOE POKE FROM RONALDO WAS ENOUGH TO WIN THE MATCH. RONALDO WON THE GOLDEN SHOE WITH EIGHT GOALS, THE MOST SINCE GERD MULLER'S TEN IN 1970

AHN JUNG-HWAN HEADS THE EXTRA TIME GOAL FOR SOUTH KOREA THAT ELIMINATED ITALY. SHADES OF 1966 AND ITALY'S DEFEAT BY NORTH KOREA

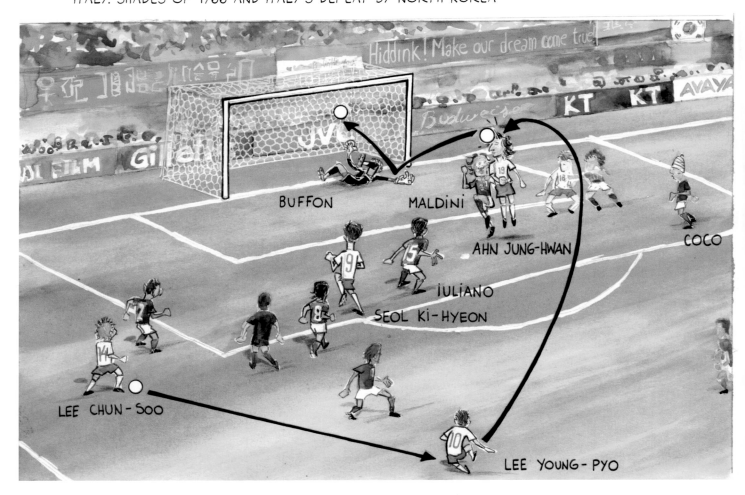

GERMANY'S MICHAEL BALLACK RECEIVES A YELLOW CARD AFTER A FOUL
ON SOUTH KOREA'S LEE CHUN-SOO. IT WAS HIS SECOND IN THE LATTER
STAGES WHICH MEANT HE MISSED THE FINAL. BUT FOUR MINUTES LATER HE
MADE SURE GERMANY GOT THERE WHEN IN THE 75TH MINUTE HE SCORED
THE ONLY GOAL OF THE GAME

BRAZIL WORLD CUP WINNERS 2002 (BACK ROW, LEFT TO RIGHT) LUCIO, EDMILSON, ROQUE JUNIOR,
GILBERTO SILVA, MARCOS,

(FRONT) RONALDINHO, RONALDO, ROBERTO CARLOS, KLEBERSON, RIVALDO, CAFU

FASTEST EVER WORLD CUP GOAL

HAKAN SUKUR SCORES THE FASTEST GOAL IN WORLD CUP HISTORY IN THE THIRD-PLACE MATCH EVEN THOUGH SOUTH KOREA KICKED OFF!

HAKAN SUKUR 10.8 SECONDS

LUIZ FELIPE SCOLARI - "BIG PHIL" - THE BRAZILIAN COACH

THE FINAL 30 June 2002
GERMANY 0 - 2 BRAZIL
International Stadium, Yokohama
Attendance: 69,029
Referee: Pierluigi Collina (Italy)

BALLACK CAN
ONLY WATCH

49th minute

SO CLOSE...

OLIVER NEUVILLE HIT THE POST
WITH A GREAT SHOT FROM
30 YARDS

SPLAT!

OLIVER KAHN FUMBLES A LOW SPECULATIVE SHOT FROM RIVALDO

PLOF!

1-0   AND RONALDO STRIKES FOR THE
       FIRST GOAL

67th minute

2-0   RONALDO

79th minute

BRAZIL CHAMPIONS AGAIN!!!

2006 GERMANY

THE WORLD CUP'S MOST INFAMOUS MOMENT. THE RED MIST ENVELOPES ZINEDINE ZIDANE AND HE HEADBUTTS MARCO MATERAZZI. A RED CARD FOLLOWED AND A GREAT CAREER ENDED IN IGNOMINY

2006 GERMANY

SURELY IT WAS A SAFE BET that the Germans would win the World Cup when it was staged in their own country? But German football was going through a transitional phase and it was two other European powers, France and Italy, who contested the final.

And the result was a fourth win for the Azzurri in a match which had an astonishing finale when the world's greatest player, Zinedine Zidane, appeared to self-destruct.

Germany had to be content with third place after they appeared to realise they did not have the talent to grind down the opposition as they had in the past. They appointed their former flamboyant striker, Jürgen Klinsmann, as coach and played flowing attacking football. They were top scorers with 14 goals.

The reigning champions Brazil flattered to deceive. Despite their stars it seemed their old European inferiority complex had returned once again.

It was the mighty who lined up in the last 16. And it was the mighty who by and large went through to the last eight, although Portugal first had to sort out the Netherlands 1-0 in a match which saw 16 yellow cards, with four players being sent off for second bookable offences.

Portugal met England in the last eight in a match disfigured by the sending off of Wayne Rooney after an hour, winning a penalty shoot-out.

France, meanwhile, were gathering momentum. Zidane belied his 33 years to see off Spain, Brazil and Portugal on their way to the final.

Italy, showing great teamwork and commitment despite dispiriting thoughts of a match-fixing scandal at home, beat the Germans 2-0 in their semi-final but most fans anticipated Zidane picking up the golden cup at the end of the 4th of July match in Berlin.

But the abiding memory of Zidane was his astonishing headbutt. There had been little indication of such a cataclysmic ending as the match unwound.

The Italians could not capitalise on Zidane's absence but then it came to the penalty shoot-out and the cup was Italy's for the fourth time.

ZIDANE WALKS OFF THE PITCH AT THE BERLIN OLYMPIC STADIUM
WITHOUT A BACKWARD GLANCE AT THE TROPHY.
THE SPECTATORS CAN HARDLY BELIEVE THEIR EYES

THE ACCROBATIC MIROSLAV KLOSE.
THE GERMAN STRIKER WON THE GOLDEN SHOE WITH FIVE GOALS

RONALDO'S THREE GOALS TOOK HIS
WORLD CUP TOTAL TO 15, A RECORD.
HERE HE BAMBOOZLES GHANIAN
GOALKEEPER RICHARD KINGSON

MICHAEL BALLACK,
THE GERMAN CAPTAIN,
STRIDES OUT TO
MEET HIS PUBLIC

GERMAN GOALKEEPER JENS LEHMANN KEPT HIS NOTES ABOUT ARGENTINA'S PENALTY TAKERS IN HIS SOCK. HE SAVED *TWICE* IN THE SHOOT-OUT

OUCH!!!

OUCH INDEED. ENGLAND'S WAYNE ROONEY STAMPS ON THE TENDER PARTS OF PORTUGAL'S RICARDO CARVALHO. ROONEY'S THEN MANCHESTER UNITED CLUB-MATE CRISTIANO RONALDO RUSHES FORWARD IN HIGH DUDGEON...

...LATER HE WINKS TO THE PORTUGUESE BENCH AS IF TO SAY "JOB DONE. WE WOUND HIM UP"

ROBERTO CARLOS LOSES CONCENTRATION, THIERRY HENRY NIPS IN TO SCORE AND FRANCE BEAT BRAZIL 1-0 TO REACH THE SEMI-FINALS

ITALY WORLD CUP WINNERS 2006 (BACK ROW, LEFT TO RIGHT) GIANLUIGI BUFFON,
MARCO MATERAZZI, LUCA TONI, FABIO GROSSO, FRANCESCO TOTTI

Aczel

NAVARO,

THE HOSTS GO OUT AS GROSSO SCORES
ITALY'S FIRST IN THE SEMI-FINAL
AFTER 119 MINUTES

THE BALL USED IN THE FINAL

THE FINAL 9 July 2006

ITALY 1 - 1 (a.e.t) FRANCE

Penalties 5-3

Olympiastadion, Berlin
Attendance: 69,000
Referee: Horacio Elizondo (Argentina)

MARCELLO LIPPI. STEERED ITALY TO
THEIR FOURTH WORLD CUP VICTORY

0-1   ZIDANE: OFF THE BAR AND IN   7th minute

1-1   19th minute   MATERAZZI HEADER

EXTRA TIME
111th minute

THE MOMENT THAT SHOCKED THE WORLD. ZIDANE ENDS HIS STAR-STUDDED CAREER WITH AN ASSAULT ON MATERAZZI THAT SEES HIM SENT OFF...

THE SHOOT OUT. TREZEGUET HITS THE BAR!

GROSSO... GOOOOAL!!!   THE WINNER!

ITALY WORLD CHAMPIONS!

-ACZEL-

2010 SOUTH AFRICA

2010 S AFRICA

FOOTBALL CONTINUES TO SPREAD ITS WINGS, with the 2010 competition being the first to be staged in Africa. In an all-African bidding process, South Africa beat Egypt and Morocco and will stage the tournament from June 11 to July 11.

The South Africans have built three new stadiums – the Mbombela in Nelspruit, the Nelson Mandela Bay Stadium in Port Elizabeth and the Peter Mokaba Stadium in Polokwane.

The opening match and final will be held in Johannesburg at Soccer City with its capacity of 94,700.

Close to Soweto, the ground was built in 1987 but has had a major refit. It had a new upper tier and roof in time for 2010, with a new changing room area and floodlights.

FIFA must have been breathing a sigh of relief after the qualifying competition was finally over. Some of the world's greatest players were in danger of missing the tournament. But Lionel Messi will be there after Argentina beat Uruguay 1-0 in Montevideo and Cristiano Ronaldo was grateful for his team-mates in his absence as they beat Bosnia-Herzegovina 2-0 in a play-off.

France, the 1998 champions and 2006 beaten finalists, squeezed through as well, beating the Republic of Ireland thanks to a blatant handball from Thierry Henry, missed by all the officials. The Irish demanded a replay but FIFA would not bend and the men in green went away mumbling of fixes, the position of France's Michel Platini as head of UEFA and the need of FIFA to have all the big nations in South Africa.

France got lucky in their group, drawing the hosts, Mexico and Uruguay. And all the other bigger nations could hardly complain either... with the notable exception of Brazil.

England could hardly have chosen better first-round opponents than the USA, Algeria and Slovenia, while the holders Italy face Paraguay, New Zealand and Slovakia.

But as usual a couple of big names will slink home early and one of them is bound to be from Group G. The seeds, Brazil, first drew North Korea, and while they will hardly be concerned it is worth remembering 1966, the last time they took part in the tournament. Then they beat Italy and were 3-0 up against Portugal before Eusebio sprang into action. Next out for Brazil were the best team in Africa, the Ivory Coast. And if an African team is to do well in its home continent then the Cote D'Ivoire are the best bet.

Last out was Portugal, renewing acquaintance with North Korea. The World Cup always has one "Group of Death" and this time it's Group G.

  # GROUP A

SOUTH AFRICA
MEXICO
URUGUAY
FRANCE

RAFAEL MARQUEZ (MEXICO)

DIEGO FORLAN (URUGUAY)

THIERRY HENRY
(FRANCE)

AARON MOKOENA (SOUTH AFRICA)

 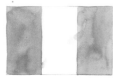 # GROUP B

ARGENTINA
NIGERIA
SOUTH KOREA
GREECE

PARK JI-SUNG (SOUTH KOREA)

NWANKWO KANU
(NIGERIA)

GIORGOS KARAGOUNIS (GREECE)

LIONEL MESSI (ARGENTINA)

  # GROUP C

ENGLAND
USA
ALGERIA
SLOVENIA

YAZID
MANSOURI
(ALGERIA)

LANDON
DONOVAN
(USA)

ROBERT KOREN
(SLOVENIA)

-ACZEL-

WAYNE ROONEY (ENGLAND)

 **GROUP D**

GERMANY
AUSTRALIA
SERBIA
GHANA

HARRY
KEWELL
(AUSTRALIA)

MICHAEL ESSIEN (GHANA)

DEJAN STANKOVIC (SERBIA)

MICHAEL BALLACK (GERMANY)

  # GROUP E

NETHERLANDS
DENMARK
JAPAN
CAMEROON

CHRISTIAN POULSEN
(DENMARK)

SHUNSUKE NAKAMURA (JAPAN)

SAMUEL ETO'O (CAMEROON)

ARJEN ROBBEN (NETHERLANDS)

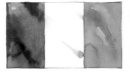  # GROUP F

ITALY
PARAGUAY
NEW ZEALAND
SLOVAKIA

RYAN NELSON (NEW ZEALAND)

NELSON VALDEZ (PARAGUAY)

MAREK HAMSIK (SLOVAKIA)

FABIO CANNAVARO (ITALY)

  # GROUP G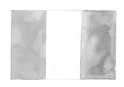

BRAZIL
NORTH KOREA
IVORY COAST
PORTUGAL

DIDIER DROGBA (IVORY COAST)

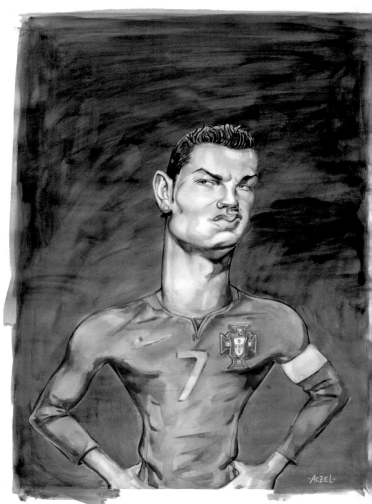

CRISTIANO RONALDO
(PORTUGAL)

HONG YONG-JO (NORTH KOREA)

KAKA (BRAZIL)

  # GROUP H

SPAIN
SWITZERLAND
HONDURAS
CHILE

ALEXANDER FREI
(SWITZERLAND)

ALEXIS SANCHEZ
(CHILE)

AMADO GUEVARA (HONDURAS)

FERNANDO TORRES (SPAIN)

GERMAN ACZEL IS AN ARGENTINIAN ARTIST WHO NOW LIVES IN MUNICH IN GERMANY. AFTER WINNING PRIZES IN HIS NATIVE BUENOS AIRES, HE BEGAN WORKING FOR ARGENTINA'S MOST IMPORTANT NEWSPAPER, *LA NACION*, MOVING ON TO THE COUNTRY'S BIGGEST SPORTS MAGAZINE, *EL GRAFICO*. HE WAS 20 WHEN HE HAD HIS FIRST EXHIBITION AND HE HAS REPRESENTED ARGENTINA IN MANY OVERSEAS EXHIBITIONS. AFTER WORKING IN BRAZIL FOR *JORNAL DO BRASIL*, HE MOVED TO EUROPE AT 26, MEETING HIS WIFE JOHANNA WHEN DANCING THE TANGO IN MUNICH. HE NOW WORKS FOR *BRAVO SPORT MAGAZINE*.

DEDICATED TO MY CHILDREN:
LUCIANO, PATRICIO AND LEONARDO

Published in Great Britain by
SportsBooks Limited
PO Box 422
Cheltenham
GL50 2YN
United Kingdom

Tel: 01242 256755
Fax: 0560 3108126
email: info@sportsbooks.ltd.uk
www.sportsbooks.ltd.uk

© Drawings: German Aczel 2010
    Text: Randall Northam 2010
    Design: Alan Hunns Graphics

A catalogue record for this book is available from the British Library.

ISBN 9781899807857

Printed in China
on behalf of Latitude Press Ltd